I0192022

Preface

[Type here]

Many of the ideas in this book are not my own but were given to me as I wrote. I do not claim this book is "divinely inspired" but as all writers must find "inspiration" I have no other way to express the possession of my being in the creative process but as being inspired by something outside of myself which worked through me in connection with the word creating a fervor and a passion to complete this book in a week.

There is a section where I specifically draw attention to the fact that I am giving my own possible interpretation as to something particular in relation to the Genesis account. In fact, anytime I diverge from the realm of inspiration I clearly state it.

In my own interpretations of the Genesis account the theories I submit to the reader are no more absurd than the idea of all intelligent and conscious life as coming as a result of evolving from the aggregation of elements into a single cell (which happened to form randomly) out of a great ocean of primordial ooze, over 4 billion years ago and then formed itself together in haphazard series of

[Type here]

evolutionary events out of the all the infinity of all possible scenarios into not just one a being, but thousands of living things all of which are not only physically symmetrical in every aspect but one in particular being able to not only being capable of comprehending its own existence but also the existence of its creator and a relationship to that creator.

What the reader can expect from this book

1. A thesis as to why suffering and deception exists

2. How the sensory organs of sight and hearing are used as tools to infect us with a proclivity towards a darkness of the soul a desire to be ignorant.

3. A view which is divergent from main stream Christianity and still maintaining a faith based perspective

4. Mentally sticky concepts which will challenge the reader's understanding and assumptions and beliefs of modern religion.

[Type here]

What the reader should NOT expect

1. "Scientific" data and analysis given in statistics and in an effort to prove something according to world "consensus"

2. Perfectly written prose in elegant fashion, (sometimes the sentences are run on sentences but the ideas must be written in that way to present the full concept.

3. Told what to believe. What you choose to believe is yours to own

[Type here]

Introduction

If you don't accept the Bible as the ultimate authority of God's word, then put this book down and walk away.

I use the Bible as one of my only sources to explain different ideas- not to prove to people that God exists, but to share a new thought paradigm with people of faith who already know he exists. I rely on little other material to explain the concepts in this book. I am acting according to my faith in Our Lord Jesus being the word and God's authority as final.

[Type here]

This book is not written to convert anyone to any religion or prove my ideas. I make no claim to be a prophet of God or to possess revelatory insight of mind. I hold no degree in any field and hold no certifications in Theology.

I am just a believer who wants to share from inspiration. In this book I suggest there is a reality in which we can experience a much more intimate relationship with our Creator and his son which can manifest into a shared reality.

I am at most a child of God more so a babe in Christ. I do not call myself a Christian because that word immediately implies the denominational and doctrinal based divisions of man-made churches of Earth. My position is that I am a believer in the body of Christ and his sacrifice, resurrection, and ascension for the remission of our sins by the act of his propitiation. The statement is made to express the totality of my faith and of belief, there is no need to ask what denomination I am or if I believe Jesus Is God or if I believe baptism is necessary for the remission of sins or to justify any specific doctrine according to the need to fit into the Earthly

[Type here]

standard. My authority is our Lord and Savior Christ Jesus, my doctrine is his way of truth.

There are more than 40 different English of versions of the Bible in America today. Clearly the word of God has been fragmented by something. The specific version of the Bible I use is the King James version and the reasons for that will explain in the later chapters.

Part of my thesis is that the current model of religion is built to conform to manufactured divisions which have not the goal to bring strengthen the body of Christ but only serve to line the pockets of so-called Church leaders and in fact weaken our faith.

The many leaders of non-profit religious institutions have for-profit business entities that operate for the church leaders to make money. We will take a closer look at that in Chapter 5. I make every effort to use scripture to supplement points and do my best to avoid injecting what is considered mainstream

[Type here]

opinions or scholarly consensus as defined by the world system of associations such as a Baptist Association, Pentecostal association, Episcopalian association. In addition, there is not any kind of scholarly association or political association I am a part of. I believe the roots of our faith of our faith have not just been pulled up and thrown into the air but scattered and divided throughout all manner of religious organizations. It is through the manipulation of our memories and the continuation of deception not only through the institutions of the world, but many of our church leaders as well, that our faith-based lives been corrupted.

For as it is written "Behold, I send you forth as sheep in the midst of wolves be ye therefore wise as serpents and harmless as doves". Mathew 10:16. In today's world the only sure way to defeat evil is through awareness of the deception using wisdom, not physical force or aggression. Perhaps this is why Solomon says in Proverbs 4:7" Wisdom is the principal thing; therefore, get wisdom and with all thy getting, "get understanding".

[Type here]

As it is written a house divided against itself cannot stand and no man is able to serve two masters equally with devotion of will. Believers in Christ should be one of mind and one soul. We are to be subjects of a Unity of faith in the final authority being that of Christ Jesus. If we continue to deceive ourselves by the imaginations of the world system, we can't achieve this.

The divisions that exist among our faith continue to propagate a lack of coherence which results in a lack of unity of faith multiplying the division of souls.

This book will raise questions more than other books on faith-based subjects which have a relation to religion and Christianity in general. We seldom question or ask anything anymore. In fact, the internet has become the main authority on most subjects. Technology has taken the position of the new priesthood which is not a priesthood of light and truth but a priesthood which seeks to exalt itself by use of light to godhood through deception.

[Type here]

Why is it when we are in Sunday school it is a class structure but when we become adults it becomes a "service" in which one person is standing doing all the talking? Even the disciples with Jesus asked questions and had dialogues in their learning process. In fact, if we read most of the accounts of their interactions with Jesus it is always like they are in Sunday school. If we don't A.S.K then we aren't asking, seeking or knocking. In fact, we shouldn't be asking men too many questions about God, we should be asking God himself. There is too much blind devotion given to church leaders and not enough questioning from the body of believers. To sit in churches closed mouth while listening to someone talking isn't doing anything for the growth of our souls. It's no different from a business meeting. The people in the congregation remain in silence without being able to ask questions or raise points as compunction directs them to gain understanding. On the other hand, there are churches where the congregations shout and yell things like "amen" and "preach it brother" or "that's right" as if these are validations of truth as to the veracity of what the preacher is saying and it's a show.
[Type here]

These church leaders only explain concepts which they think are relevant and they are only conveying what they believe to be true. Why is authority of a singular person being taken as truth when little is shared as a whole? Truth comes from reflection. I do not propose in using some Socratic or Greek philosophical methodology to arrive at a truth, (however those are very effective measures) and using logic is an appropriate means to arrive at some relative truths. And as the head of our spiritual body is Jesus whose is the logos of God, from which we get the word logic. Logic would be a good starting point to begin our journey. But if logic *doesn't* lead to enough reflection to a degree where revelation of the word is revealed then it's just another kind of worldly knowledge. Accordingly, the logos which is Christ Jesus as the head our body therefore implies using some sort of reasoning method as a tool to arrive at greater awareness which fosters wisdom. But our wisdom as believers is premised in faith on the acknowledgment of a Creator known as God and as often quoted "Fear of the Lord is the beginning of knowledge, but fools despise wisdom and instruction.". Later in the book we

[Type here]

will see how relevant the second half the statement is especially regarding willing ignorance.

We already possess the spirit of life by virtue of having life breathed into us at our formation. Genesis 2:7 "And the lord God formed man of the dust of the ground and breathed into him and man became a living soul". So logically speaking we should consider our purpose here is to realize the soul of God. The only way God's Soul can be realized is through the acceptance in the soul of Jesus, as Jesus said John in14:6 "I am the way and the truth and the life. No one comes to the father except through me". The key word here is through, being joined to the body of Christ is not to be joined in spirit, as we were already given the spirit at formation to become not just a soul, but a "living soul "Genesis Ch.2: 7.

It is to take part in the very nature and essence of the soul of Jesus to truly understand what it means to be in the body of Christ. To be a member of the body of Christ is to access his soul which is given by God to us through his sacrifice. As consciousness comes from the soul so too does Christ

[Type here]

Consciousness come from God's soul. Much is spoken about God's spirit but much less is spoken of regarding his soul. People often use the terms spirit and soul interchangeably, like placeholders or synonyms but they are clearly defined as different in Genesis chapter 2:7 "And the Lord God formed man of the dust of the ground and breathed into his nostrils the breath of life and man became a living soul". This clearly shows there is a distinct difference. What is the difference between a soul and a living soul? And why can the body live without a soul but not without a spirit? We shall explore these ideas later in the book.

Your perceptions and understanding will be challenged by some of the ideas I propose. And I believe there are others out there who have asked the same questions as I ask and have had similar ideas. I hope by writing this book I can show at least one person you are not alone in your personal revelations and there is another who shares your mind.

This book is arranged in a progressive order designed to slowly address specific concepts which will lead to an

[Type here]

awareness which I sincerely hope will provide richer and more vibrant insight, and a new way to approach the understanding of what it means to be a faith walker.

In addition, the veil of deception and reality of intentional misinformation will be torn asunder to reveal the nature of what we are facing in the war on not only mankind but our world and the spirit of God.

This book is divided into six chapters:

Chapter 1

What is revelation? Seeing and perceiving. The difference between seeing with eyes and discerning through insight. Seeing through deception of the material world and perceiving with the soul to understand the soul of that which is being

[Type here]

seen.

Chapter 2

The role willing ignorance plays in the world as related to deception and how it corrupts our faith as believers in the word. God and Lucifer's role in this unfolding drama.

Chapter 3

The relationship between revelation and ignorance and understanding the dynamics of hearing and the role it plays in the development of our faith-based life.

Chapter 4

The Genesis account through a different lens. Establishing a new possible foundation of understanding in the first two accounts of the creation process which leads to a paradigm shift in our perception of God and creation.

[Type here]

Chapter 5

Where did the need to prove or create certain doctrines and principles regarding Salvation and God's word come from?

Chapter 6

Why do bad things happen? Exploring God's role behind the creation of suffering and pain in our lives and how it can transform us.

[Type here]

Chapter one

Where does Revelation come from?

Eyes to see and ears to hear is often a phrase used throughout the New Testament by Christ. Either he was a very

[Type here]

redundant person or just had to remind himself of the functions of the human body. Neither of the two scenarios make much sense considering his stature and Power in the universe. Often, Jesus spoke of mysteries and spoke in metaphors-for his own reasons. So, what does it mean to have eyes and not see? All of us can understand this as looking at something and yet not realizing what it is we are looking at, that is, not seeing what it really is. Often, we hear people say "appearances can be deceiving" or I can't make out what that is, or even what am I looking at? The Simplicity and profundity of the words to see something but not know what you are looking at is something we all take for granted. How precious is the gift of sight. To see the world around you is a marvelous gift, but interestingly, if a person is blind there other.

senses become so heightened that their power of perception reaches almost mystical proportion. And in some circumstances a blind person has better discernment as to the nature of something right in front of them which they cannot see more so than a person with perfectly good sight. There is a

[Type here]

difference between true vision and sight. This is proof that the powers of discernment come from more than just the organ of observation or rather more than an organ for observation. We live in a world of technology in which we see things constantly. We are bombarded daily with visual images which blind the eyes like a dull yet persistent flash from a camera always before our eyes. It is happening at such a degree that a lot of people walk around in true perceptual blindness, only able to see what is in front of their face. And often, forgetting what they were just looking at because of the endless stream of visual noise. Whether it be television, cell phones or computers we are constantly bombarded with visual images. From the beginning of transmissible technology, the printing press and the advent of the written word when books began to be published and newspapers began to circulate creating newspaper companies which began to flourish, we have constantly had something before our eyes and in front of our face to look at and 2000 years ago, it wasn't so. Our senses of perceiving from visual sight have been obfuscated for the last 500 years not only physically but on a level which has

[Type here]

penetrated our souls to the degree where forgetting is in our DNA. When we watch the news or look at a computer or use our cell phones what are we really seeing? Is this visual gluttony guiding us more and more to a state where the human soul is becoming anemic? So how does the idea of having a revelatory experience into seeing and being able to perceive with true discernment fit in to this world of blinding light and rapid displays of images which are constantly assaulting our visual acuity?

In Scripture Paul says that when he saw the resurrected Christ on the Damascus Road it blinded him for 3 days. in Acts chapter 9 verses 3 to 9 we see how Paul's experience on the road to Damascus led him to have a revelatory experience. The resurrected Christ appears to Paul and talks to him but before that happens a blinding light strikes Paul and Paul loses his sight. For 3 days he could not see, he literally had no sight. It is interesting in that passage that Ananias receives a vision, but Paul loses his sight. Clearly there is something going on with one man losing his sight and the other man receiving a vision. This demonstrates how interconnected the power of

[Type here]

perception and vision are to discernment. And of course, everyone knows what happened next, Paul had a transformation, he went through a spiritual growth he went through a soulical growth.

How many times have you seen a movie and then watched it again later a second time and thought "Hey I didn't see that the first time I watched that movie". So even though you watched a movie and you saw it, the first time you saw it you were figuratively speaking blind the big picture until the second time you watched it. So, the first time we could say that seeing you perceived it not. This is a superficial example but it's something to which we can all relate. And when you watch it the second time there is always something you see which you missed the first.

The same thing happens with our relationship dynamics when interacting with people. As we see our friends and learn about them, we understand them more and more and we can know them better. It is through repeated interaction with something that we can learn to perceive what makes them unique. Only seeing something one time will not create a deeper

[Type here]

understanding or an opportunity to have a deeper understanding of it. So, the importance of understanding something comes from knowledge but it's a knowledge based on frequency of interactions that occur more than one time. To know somebody better means more than to just have an awareness of them. We can know of a person but not actually know them. Having knowledge of a thing creates an awareness to it if we have an awareness to it, we can get some knowledge about it and then understand it and come to know it better. We can gain an insight about its essence. An insight not based only upon what we see or the appearance of it but what we perceive by looking into it and through it when we use our vision to perceive it.

 In scripture the books of Daniel Ezekiel Isaiah and Jeremiah as well as Revelations are most often associated with the idea of Prophecy. And of course, revelatory experience. In many churches prophecy is associated with revelation. To say the prophets in those scriptures had revelations would be a very redundant statement   and there have been hundreds of interpretations of these prophecies over the years so I won't
[Type here]

attempt any kind of explanation of them as that isn't the purview of this book. One thing that all of them have in common is that they all reflected about their relationship with God. They prayed for the reason of active communion on a *frequent* basis. They weren't watching Hebrew tube or surfing babel net in their free time. Often, they really didn't have much say in the matter of whether or not they would have roles as prophets, but they all listened because they could hear. They also *accepted* what God wanted of them out of willingness, not out of a need to just obey. They prayed, they talked with God and had conversations with him. sometimes they directly asked God to show them something and sometimes it was revealed while other times it was given but in symbols or some veiled meaning which even, they struggled with. And they were much more in tune with the soul of righteousness than anyone nowadays. They must have felt comfortable and trusted him like children. This means they had a relationship and had a literally a high frequency of interaction with him. They were able to understand his nature

[Type here]

and how he communicated by spending time with him. How often do you spend time with God.?

Going to church once a week is hardly a way to *remember* the word or spend time on an intimate level with God. When you go to church you are in fact spending time listening to another person tell you about God. Not trying to listen to God himself. I am not implying that going to church is something that you should not do. The time we spend in fellowship is a gift from our father and should be sought every day. Although spending an hour putting on makeup or ironing a suit and putting on a tie to look like someone going to a model shoot or a business meeting seems more about appearance then participating in an opportunity to have a revelatory experience. If people are more preoccupied with appearance and looking at the externals; how can they have a chance to exercise their powers of perception on an intimate level with another person more-so with God? It could be said that when we are in church, we should be learning to see to perceive and train ourselves how to receive revelation but there is no

[Type here]

exercising of perception when everyone is more concerned with appearance. Fellowship is an act of participation, and it is an act of participating in Christ consciousness. And is a valuable part of our growth. It is how we participate in our community.

Today we are in of age of individuation and self-empowerment, and it seems like people can't maintain enough attention to give anything focus longer than a few minutes without looking at their cellphones. There is a lot of medication being distributed to help with "attention deficit" disorder. People have enough trouble focusing on their daily tasks and there is there is very little room for the acknowledgment of God and a desire to see him daily and much less a need to serve God. All our technology has taken all the external information we process daily beyond our sense data realm and into our very consciousness. In fact, it is pulling us deeper everyday into an abyss of the unknown, it is no wonder why our world is getting darker and darker.

[Type here]

There is so much visual noise that what we are looking at is obscured and our perception of spiritual discernment through the faculty of sight is full of static much like the old days when we used rabbit ears to try and dial into a good frequency in order to clear the picture on a TV from all the snow. In fact, one can draw very accurate parallel to communication with God among all the visual distractions we are bombarded with daily to watching a TV program which is cluttered with white noise. The lack of being able to perceive or spiritually discern is detrimental to our souls. It affects our ability to experience revelation not only regarding scriptural knowledge but knowledge of and into the nature of things and people, but it also affects our own self-reflection. How often do you take the time in your day to open yourself up to revelation, which is a revelation regarding your own nature? How often do you have a chance to consider why you do or say what you do and how it affects yourself and others? Are you even aware of what you are doing throughout your day? We often verbalize decisions of our past which we made using conditionals such as if. If I would not have done that, or, if only I did this. If I get this

[Type here]

much money, I want to buy this, or if I don't get that job how can I pay this bill? and on and on it goes. These are kinds of reflections that offer only daydreams of alternate realities that could have been or might be with no real effect on how our future will be or how we make choices for our futures. Unless we take the time to search our innermost being and have acceptance and patience to sit and give ourselves the attention necessary to ask why we do what we do or why we say what we say, there will never be a manifestation revelation of truth about who we are.

As Believers we must acknowledge that the cornerstone of being in the body of Christ is truth. For our Christ is truth and if we don't open our souls up to what that means in regard to us personally, we will not be able to access the gifts given to us by the holy soul. It is interesting that the word holy means something set apart for a specific purpose or reason. And how does that relate to believers in the body of Christ? If we are truly filled with the soul which has been set apart, we must ask ourselves set apart from what? In scripture we read we" do

[Type here]

not conform to the image of the world". I can only see one way, one truth and one life that can grant the ability to do this. That is being filled with Christ Consciousness which means not conforming to the image of the world is a function of. We must be in the world but not be of it, that means accepting but not comprising, innocent but not naive, harmless but wise. In a material world blending is one of the most important skills for survival. And that creates problems for believers. How can we fit in without being corrupted? I don't have an answer for that question other than Proverbs 1:7 "the fear of the lord is the beginning of wisdom". My only suggestion is making God real in your life by asking him to draw near to you and be in your life. It sounds like some flaky Christian thing to say and to that I reply-So?

I don't have all the answers but if one begins the process of true self-reflection the answers will come, and solutions will manifest in a way that is unique and specific to you. I am giving you the golden key to your cage, believe in this and accept it. Your life will change if you actively engage in this

[Type here]

process... How does one reflect? At this point there are probably people thinking this guy isn't really saying something new. My hope is to increase awareness to the necessity of the function of asking to manifest revelation in each person's life daily, not to say something new but to build an awareness to a new way of looking at things for members of the body of Christ. And in discussing reflection it's necessary to distinguish reflection from prayer or meditation. What does it mean to reflect? How does one reflect? Is reflecting the same as standing in front of a mirror and looking at yourself? Not exactly and yet in a way it is. You use your soul as a mirror to see your physical self and all your deeds and actions which you have done throughout the day. You watch yourself from the perspective of immaterial self.

   The best example I can give is Leonardo Da Vinci. It has been said that at night before sleeping while in bed, Leonardo Da Vinci revisited every event which happened in his daily activities, every interaction was looked at objectively and processed in a non-biased way. I am not saying to obsess over

[Type here]

your every activity at night before going to bed. Obsessing is a form of bringing your thoughts into your consciousness as calcified attachments to things that bother you like a barnacle on a ship in the ocean. Reflecting is the opposite it requires only the opening of the heart to the truth of your behavior and your motivations regarding what you did that day in the dynamics of your interactions with people during your day. It is very much like a mental diary. But we aren't limited to pen and paper we can approach it much like a quantum computer and the process requires to only be willing, open and truthful with oneself. For where truth is revelation can manifest. When one can perceive the truth of their behavior and the motivations for it a new dimension of growth begins to emerge, and this is the entry into the domain of the Holy Soul.

We use the term conscience a lot to describe the innate sense of right and wrong. There's a lot of talk in every church I go to about obeying. And how the conscience will "convict" us regarding what is right and what is wrong because we must obey God and it is "through our conscience that he speaks to

[Type here]

us to us. The voice of conscience is the voice of conscience, it is just you talking to yourself from a moralistic view. Do you really think obeying our own conscience will solve every problem that we have in life. There are times when following what a person thinks is right can get them in prison by breaking the law. So conscience is not something that will not solve the dilemma of knowing right and wrong. "Obey God's word, obey the law obey obey, obey" as if just obeying will solve every problem that is in society.

Everyone has a conscience and yet people still do bad things and people do bad things and acknowledge it while they're doing it. Even if somebody obeys the law today, they might not obey the law tomorrow. If somebody is operating not out of willingness but out of fear of being punished, then what happens when that threat of punishment is taken away? When there are no restrictions will they still choose to obey even if there's no punishment or will they have conscience enough to convict them of doing what is "right" and not what is "wrong"? Sometimes guilt gets the better of a person

[Type here]

before they act on a thought, and they have an awareness of the harm they might do. And yet some people do bad things repeatedly even if the law and their conscience are against it.

Those kinds of people could said to be soulless. But we know from scripture we all became a living soul. For what is conscience if not the soul that starts at birth and grows in capacity to experience the range of emotions in our human lives? We are all already of one spirit. The breath of life is the spirit of God, but our souls are the domain of the sum of our choices which arise from our consciousness not our conscience. For if we do good out of the need to obey then is it really doing good or helping our soul to grow? A soldier obeys, a soldier follows orders, and a soldier does what he is told and doesn't think about it. And through that obedience gains rank. But that means his soul grows. Gaining rank and authority is how many church leaders today get into positions of authority. And then they frequently mention obedience as this is the way by which knowledge their souls grew. In the course of time the soul does grow but there those that are

[Type here]

willingly ignorant, and this is an entirely different mindset. Or it could grow much more if they could realize that what they think the see is more about how they have been taught to see. They have a soul, but it has been deceived and the sense of self, the sense of being right because some group or institution says you are right.

This system of authority has exalted itself to the degree that even the possibility of to the awareness of something won't give knowledge of it and this includes God. As a result of the information age, ironically, willing ignorance has become the driving force of the world now more than at any other age in human history. As we learn in Proverbs1:7 "The fear of the lord is the beginning of knowledge, but fools despise wisdom and instruction". If there is no respect of God than the understanding is only able to go as far as far as the knowledge allows it. So, the ability to grow, which often means suffering through the reality of the shame of being wrong. As we were given free will our role in this life is not to be as a soldier and just obey. For it was Jesus that willingly gave his life for the

[Type here]

world, and it was God our Father in Heaven who willingly gave his son to be a sacrifice.

Obeying is something that men tell others to do when they have no real justification for them to be doing it. It is interesting to know that in churches often the idea of being obedient and doing what God says is usually followed by the passing of the plate for tithing and offerings. It is a simple thing to understand the purpose of tithing. But tithing is a process of following a prescribed expectation out of a need to obey a precept. Tithing is done by many people with the expectation that if they give something they will get something, and this is not the nature of the soul of giving. The idea of giving a tenth of what you have is a lesson to teach us by learning to give something small in the material realm we will come to know the joy of selfless by growing more into the nature of his soul and experiencing joy from selfless acts. Matthew 6:19-21 "Store up for yourselves treasures in heaven. "Do not store up for yourselves treasures on earth, where moth and rust destroy and where thieves break in and

[Type here]

steal". Jesus connects this statement to the idea that "Where your treasure is, there your heart will be also" (Matthew 6:21) For it is the joy of sharing which results from the blessing of giving. So Tithing is about experiencing the Joy of sharing. It's not done to get something in return. But there are thousands of believers who really think that if they give money, they will get financial abundance. As Jesus took joy in his suffering so that we could be forgiven and redeemed we should take joy in sharing not only our money but our time. The only time I truly feel fulfilled is when I give of myself, in fact it could be said that I'm not addicted to anything but giving. As far as addictions go this is not a bad addiction to have although sometimes it can be to my detriment. And I always remember Jesus words "let your moderation be known to all men".

I have no idea what asking for money has to do with drawing near to God for manifesting the soul of Christ within a congregation. But I do know that there are two things that don't belong in the house of God, they are wallets and cell phones. Many churches have "gift shops" where the ministers

[Type here]

or pastors have books in which they sell books or videos…This I cannot abide. I can't imagine Jesus running around a stage with a headset on or standing in front of podium or in a pulpit preaching about the hell fire and damnation of the sinners and unjust. The next time you see your church leader at service watch him and ask yourself is this a man Jesus would have allowed to be a disciple? That is a very high bar, but we serve the highest God. It is true that churches need to pay for repairs and pay for bills and there are employees of churches which get paid salaries. But I can't help but wonder, maybe if we changed our idea of how to worship and grow in Christ these problems would be minimized. But if a church needs to ask for money to pay bills or pay the paychecks …it is a kind of conformance to the image of the world. The longer we keep accepting that "this is the way it is" the longer it will keep going. It's time for us to not hope but expect our head to return. Stop hoping and wishing and start asking Christ Jesus to return. We are to be in the world but not of it. If we are in the body of Christ but we are simultaneously acting in the image of the world there is a problem with how we as

[Type here]

believers in Christ perceive reality. We should be praying in our congregations every time we are together in one voice and in one hope with sincere expectation and with a mature, sober mindset asking him to return. I don't mean emotional outbursts and yelling "praise Jesus" and making outward displays of dramatic behavior. According to Mathew 6 we are to pray by making a display Mathew 6:5 " And when thou prayest, thou shalt not be as the hypocrites are: for they love to pray standing in the synagogues and in the corners of the streets that they may be seen of men". I doubt the apostles were running around handling snakes and speaking gibberish or shouting and yelling things when Jesus was teaching. Our true faith needs to return and this fake churchianity needs to disappear. I call it fake because it is. I would like someone to explain to me the numerous church leaders who have planes and expensive cars and multiple mansions and have affiliations with business conglomerates.

Contrary to the idea of money being the root of all evil it seems to me evil is the root of all evil. Money in and of itself is

[Type here]

inert; it has no life it's like blaming money for the existence of evil. Evil has existed long before money and mankind. So, it follows money and evil have no real relationship aside from it being a tool used by the deceiver to manifest the soul of greed or corruption or a distraction. It can be used as well for giving and helping and manifesting the soul of goodness. When talking about money there are truly two sides to every coin.

2, 000 years ago when people used seashells to trade and buy and barter, I doubt anyone would have said that seashells are the root of all evil. This kind of metaphor is an example of how deception is used to make people blind. It actually comes from one Timothy chapter 6 verse 10 which says, "For the Love of Money is the root of all kinds of evil." So, as we can see money is just a tool which can be used to manifest different kinds of influences.

If you haven't put the book down yet I appreciate your diligence and your gift of attention. As we have seen revelation comes from truth which can only be found in reflection. From appreciation of and desire to draw near to

[Type here]

truth we enter a Christ Consciousness which leads to a sense of community and love for one another. For we are already of one spirit but different minds. It is the spirit of God which binds our souls to our bodies as in Genesis chapter 2 verse 7" then the Lord God formed a man from the dust of the ground and breathed into his nostrils the Breath of Life, and Man became a living soul." So, we see in scripture the truth that there is a distinction between spirit and soul. Spirit is the Breath of God it is what animates and gives life to everything. All things that breathe, all things that live, all things that exist by and through the spirit God.

But it only becomes real with acknowledging God. To most people this means simply saying, Oh Sure I believe in God I go to a church. But what do you do the rest of the time? Where is your heart throughout the day? I have seen go to church and 10 minutes later they are using hand gestures to articulate an explicative in traffic. Forgetting is a dangerous thing.

In Scripture it is written that many false prophets will arrive after our Lord departs. On social media platforms we can see

[Type here]

an endless supply of people claiming to have some special insights revelation into the mind of God and what he wants from us. It's a pretty simple thing to understand what God wants from us. He wants our love and affection, and he wants us to know him and draw close to him. He wants to give love to others so his soul can fill the Earth.

To dispute whether Jesus Is God or the Son of God or both or not or whether or not you need to be baptized in order to go to heaven is to miss the entire meaning of Jesus's message, and Its petty, but this is part of the soul of deception that we are living with in the world and it has been in existence since Adam and Eve were first formed. I say all that to plainly say the problem with Bible scholar experts is that they don't know what they don't know and won't admit when they could be wrong because they have too much invested in perpetuating the deception. I would suggest that believers be wary of any church leader who has the answers to all your questions.

Most of the answers can and will be revealed to you by asking, that is asking seeking and knocking. But there are limits

[Type here]

to what we are able to know. For example It is not appointed for any man to know the date or the time of the end. As Jesus said he would come as a thief in the night, if Jesus said this how can any man claim to know the hour or the time? Why would anyone follow someone who claims to know when clearly Jesus said otherwise. And that is their being in God. In Act 17:28 we read" For in him we live and move and have our being". The spirit of God is in everything that has life, for it is in him that we move and have our being, but it is through us that his spirit moves and has its being multiplied. And from that spirit things can be revealed to you not only about you but for you.

In genesis Chapter 2:7 we were given a living soul. And it is also through the world that all life has Its being. There is no air in space. Have you ever reflected on the implications of this? God is not only the essence of air and breath he is life itself, without the spirit of God there can be no life to join the soul to the body. There is no need to worship nature or the stars because his glory is all around and through everything. The

[Type here]

only thing we need to do is draw near to him is to acknowledge him; he will do the rest. It is so very simple. The soul is given at conception. It begins to form as a seed like a plant, it grows like a plant; it needs air and water and light. In short it needs love. And as a plant the soul can take in something harmful and create the elements necessary for life to breathe. As the saying goes "if life gives you lemons make lemonade". Jesus was able to take the sins of the world and absorb them and then release his soul into the world for us to draw from and have eternal life. Perhaps this why he is known as the Tree of life.

Our souls are growing daily but to what end? The growth starts from the beginning, but the process is the goal of the end. It is the Alpha and the Omega. The goal is contained in the becoming. We need love to come to the awareness and knowledge of truth in order to receive revelation about our natures and in so doing come to understand his nature. We grow according to our truths and truth grows according to our knowledge, understanding and wisdom. And as "The fear of

[Type here]

the Lord is the beginning of wisdom" Psalms 111:10 we as members of the body of Christ willingly reverence him and give him glory. For me, it is not the fear of the Lord, it is the love of the Lord which is the beginning of wisdom.

It is appropriate that the first man that had a living soul should have the responsibility of tilling the ground and living in a garden. For as the Creator wanted to form man in his image, he did so with a desire that man would understand his essence. The responsibility of man being in the garden was to till the garden to keep it and to dress it; in short to nurture life and to understand growth. The revelation of the true nature of something is not a thing which we receive by trying to bring our mind to it "Consider the lilies of the field, how they grow; they toil not, neither do they spin" appearing in both Luke 12:22-32 and Matthew 6:25-34. The verse continues, "Yet I say unto you, that even Solomon in all his glory was not arrayed like one of these". How could Solomon as wise and marvelous as he was, not be more glorious in comparison to something as insignificant as a Lily? Possibly because the Lily doesn't need

[Type here]

to "do" anything except be in the presence of God's glory and does what it was meant to do with no thought or effort. It freely accepts life and freely grows without doing anything other than being to earn it. There is a relationship with God telling Moses when Moses asks him who is and God replies, "I am". The reply of I am, with the idea of just being has a close parallel. There are more than likely other associations you are making, especially about God being found in silence by Elijah. But that is something I will leave you to reflect on in your own way.

There are people who spend years going to school and studying to get a PhD in Theology. This is admirable and I have respect for them. But how does studying God a man-made institution and taking tests have to do with the fear of the Lord? Theology means the study of God, and while that is partially true, (as all deceptions are) what it really means is the study of God according to the knowledge of the world. Taking tests in order to be recognized as having credentials enough for being qualified to explain how God works is not what the apostles did. And for those who say I am living in the past; I
[Type here]

say God's word is as relevant today as it was back then and should be even more-so. The idea of changing values which come from Our Lord to fit into the world image and be more modern is not an excuse to look at scripture "from modern viewpoint". It is an excuse to compromise. This is adding and taking away from the meaning of God's word. As already mentioned, God's revelation is premised on acknowledgment of him first, knowledge of him second understanding of him thirdly and at last he gives wisdom, at no point does Scripture say go to college and learn about God. There are those who will berate me or assume that I don't value education and to this I have to say, "as you like".

Without education we wouldn't have doctors to help us or Engineers to build bridges or Astronauts to go into space, we wouldn't have Dentists, or teach us language. All of which deal with worldly matters. So, whatever is the world's; I acknowledge as belonging to the world and necessary to the world realm because these things need to be taught by someone. But God doesn't need anyone to teach his word

[Type here]

because Jesus and his apostles already did that. It is the same scholars that tell us something and then sometime later say "Oh no current data suggests this or that". Scientists and scholars seldom just say "we were wrong" that would affect the illusion of authority the world system operates under. "Believe this now" and then later "Oh no you should believe this now". General consensus doesn't make something right just because everybody says it is. The world was flat and now It's not, consensus as authority is a prime example of conforming to the image of the world. It isn't truth for someone who went to school for 8 years and learned what an institution told them to learn and be "qualified" to be an authority of God. For it is the same reason we have different denominations. It is a deception of doctrine based on false authority. The Reformation churches manifested themselves in order to protest being told what to believe and how to believe it and how they should worship so they would "get to heaven". It is the soul of Christ that can teach us everything necessary.

[Type here]

We just need to acknowledge God and that is the beginning of our relationship with him. It's the same thing happening now that already happened before, Ecclesiastes 1:9 "nothing under the sun is new". Nothing has changed except the date. The deceiver has continued to manifest himself in the same form it's just a different age, so people have forgotten. Every time the body of Christ tries to free itself from the clutches of the deceiver it doesn't happen. Why? because we are here to be deceived and it is Lucifer's function to deceive us. But more on that later.

Mistaking Authority for truth is a common theme in the history of the world especially by institutions and organizations which seek to control an aspect or more than one aspect of society. Telling people how to behave or think or believe the way they want them to. In fact, the world system wants us to obey but God wants us to willingly follow. Understanding this should give you a revelation of the soul of modern-day churches and their leaders and who they truly serve. First it was the Catholic Church and then it was the Anglican Church and then it was the Protestant church and

[Type here]

Baptist Church and then they came to came to America to escape religious persecution, but the tentacles of the deceiver spread with the church when it came here and it became even more perverse. The atrocities committed not only by the Catholic Church but early churches in America with witch trials and the absurdities of what they were teaching based on their beliefs is a reflection of willing ignorance that perpetuated itself through deception. There are absurdities today which are still being taught they're just not as egregious as they once were.

The soul of deception is also changing. For example, we see so many so-called Scholars on social media and they have podcasts to present their ideas while offering a constant stream of what they think and what their opinions are in regard to the word of God. In particular is a number of people who present their information by drawing diagrams and using linguistics and special hermeneutics to explain a biblical concept. They go so far as to use astrological associations to try and illustrate so-called end-time prophecies. This is no

[Type here]

different than the Chaldeans who worshiped Stars. Any revelation given to someone in regard to the word of God would not need diagrams or special formulations or to look to constellations in order to articulate their message because the word is truth, and Our Lord Jesus is the word. Those so-called people of God must spend a lot of time arranging what they want to say and making those special pictures, it must take a lot of time to think about what they want to do and how they want to do it. In other words, it's very contrived and very man-made. Scripture is all we need. But it only becomes real with acknowledging God.

In Scripture it is written that many false prophets will arrive after our Lord departs. On social media platforms we can see an endless supply of people claiming to have some special insights into the mind of God and what he wants from us. It's a pretty simple thing to understand what God wants from us. He wants our love and affection, and he wants us to know him and draw close to him. He wants to give love to others so his soul can fill the Earth. To dispute whether Jesus Is God or the

[Type here]

Son of God or both or not or whether or not you need to be baptized in order to go to heaven is to miss the entire meaning of Jesus's message, and Its petty, but this is part of the soul of deception that we are living with in the world and it has been in existence since Adam and Eve were first formed.

I say all that to plainly say the problem with Bible scholar experts is that they don't know what they don't know and won't admit when they could be wrong because they have too much invested in perpetuating the deception. I would suggest that believers be wary of any church leader who has the answers to all your questions. Most of the answers can and will be revealed to you by asking, that is asking seeking and knocking. But there are limits to what we are able to know. It Is not appointed for any man to know the date or the time of the end. As Jesus said he would come as a thief in the night, if Jesus said this how can any man claim to know the hour or the time? Why would anyone follow someone who claims to know when clearly Jesus said otherwise. This is another example of willing ignorance as a result of years of practiced deception on

[Type here]

which we will touch on shortly. Someone who says that they know or that they can extrapolate from looking at stars, looking at current events, or reading tea leaves can foresee your future or the world future about when Jesus will return is not speaking truth and they are only saying what they think you want to hear. One of the biggest deceptions of the deceiver is the idea that we can actually know when our Lord is returning when Jesus himself plainly declares that no man can know when it will happen so stop listening to people who tell you they know or that try to point out things that happen in relation to scripture.

In fact, everything that has been happening in Scripture that could be a reflection of end times now; has been happening since Jesus left. However, in recent years there is more darkness spreading over the Earth masquerading as information when in fact it is disinformation.

We are living in the information age however during this time there has been more misinformation and deception then have ever been in the existence on the planet. The deceptions being

[Type here]

used, and distractions being implemented to create division, make us forget and divide not only as members of Christ but members of our country and our culture and the world in general include doctrine, politics, education and finance. One of the biggest contributors to this campaign of deception is the media outlets. As we've already mentioned we are being bombarded with an incessant barrage of visual stimulation daily. Technology companies are creating new and different ways to continually change how our visual world is invaded by their perception and their idea of what we should see and how we should think. The media is the vanguard in the array fighting against man representing the soul of deception on behalf of darkness.

By continually spreading conflicting views we are kept in a constant state of confusion and disorientation. And the negativity which is spreading like a virus is toxic beyond what you can believe. You don't need to watch social media or TV. You have no obligation to spend your time to give it your attention. instead of watching TV or movies or YouTube ask to

[Type here]

be led to do something different with your time. You will receive a gift which will be all the proof of what I am saying. If you want to free yourself, just ask him to help you. With all the deception and darkness spreading there is one secret that can give hope. What is behind all this unexplained and absurd behavior going on with the destruction of our youth, and country? Why are these truly absurd policies being made by people in our government? What is going on with all this drama and the rumors spread in news and social media about China and Taiwan and American and Russia and Israel and Iran? What is behind all the changes to our environment? There is no explainable reason and yet corruption and scandals are brought to light every day. The darkness is real, Lucifer is real he is under your bed waiting for you, he is behind you those nights when you are walking down the dark streets at night alone and you feel someone watching you. He wants your soul, therefore "Be sober, be vigilant; because your adversary the devil walks about like a roaring lion, seeking whom he may devour" 1 Peter 5:8.

Because the darkness is real, so then is the light. Avoid the

[Type here]

darkness and all the shadowy places that pollute the goodness of the soul not only in the physical world but virtual as well. And you will stay well ahead of the darkness. Heed this warning. And remember: if the light is real so then is Jesus and Our heavenly Father.

Remember this in the times that trouble your soul. Always remember.

[Type here]

Chapter 2

The role willing ignorance plays in the world.

Willing ignorance plays a large part in the world especially in relation to the deceiver's plan. It's been said that ignorance is bliss, however willing ignorance is something that can lead

[Type here]

to disastrous results. We've all had the experience of driving down the road and off in the distance ahead of us is a car getting ready to turn onto the road we are driving on. My mother is one of those people who think by speaking out loud she will somehow influence the other drivers will and make them follow her orders if she says them out loud. "Don't do it, don't do it, you better not do it" she'll say. Inevitably the driver will pull out onto the road at an altogether inappropriate time and not even go the speed limit. I personally don't do this in fact I have been accused of driving like an " Old Man". I drive the way I live; with consideration of those around me. There are two behaviors that can be observed which will give you insight into the character of a person. One is how they drive and the other is how they treat their parents.

 So, to continue with my previous sentence when the other driver sees my mother, they know she's there and she knows they know she's there; in fact, both of them have full awareness of each other that is- they have mutual knowledge of one another. In this situation that mutual knowledge should

[Type here]

lead to an understanding of the possible effects which can happen based on their choices. This leads to and understanding what we should do that is a right course of action. But even being in full awareness some people just pull right on out and do it knowing full well the other driver coming down the road will slow down or stop. Why would another driver willingly subject not only himself to danger but those around himself to Danger as well? What reasons does a person have to do such a thing? This is an example of being willingly ignorant. Children often exhibit this behavior, but we call it being stubborn. For whatever reason some people choose to be irresponsible and place the responsibility on to another in an effort to satisfy a desire to implement their will that is exalt themselves from pride. I have seen a couple arguing and one of the people is clearly right (usually the woman) while the other is clearly wrong and yet neither will yield or submit to the other's point. Just for the sake of not getting embarrassed people will refuse to admit their position is wrong or at least not as correct with the person or people they are arguing with. The ultimate cause of this is simple. For

[Type here]

it is from the ego that this desire to not embarrass oneself or become ashamed because they're wrong is coming from. It is a lack of humility. Everything that is mentioned in the bible happens daily in everyone's lives from the book of Genesis to the Book of Revelation. Our physical lives are truly a manifestation and a reflection of the spiritual world. This is how we can get revelation not only of scripture in regard to scripture but from scripture in regard to life and from Life in regard to life.

 It can be said that pride is the cause of willing ignorance because there is no acknowledgment in regard to respect of God, or authority. If there is no knowledge there can be no understanding and with no understanding wisdom cannot manifest. Because many brothers and sisters don't want to be embarrassed or admit that what they have believed for so many years or have been taught by those before them is not accurate or just not true. Most people will not acquiesce to the reality of wrong thinking. If you are in the body of Christ, the words "I was wrong" or "I made a mistake" should become

[Type here]

a part of your vocabulary which you should get accustomed to saying because nobody is perfected in faith or knowledge of the word. As we read in Romans verse 10 through 12. We are destined to be deceived and prone to make mistakes. Think back to the Genesis account and the very first encounter with the serpent.

 God takes these two beings who have just been brought into being with no knowledge of much other than the existence of a tree which was put in the middle of their habitation and specifically pointed out by God and told not to touch it or eat any of the fruit which it bears. They literally only have the knowledge that there was one thing that they should not do. God takes these two innocent naive people and puts them in a beautiful paradise and says enjoy life but let me point out this tree, come check it out, look at it, but don't partake of it in any way. No word creates instant attraction to something more than the word "don't". Then he allows a being known specifically for deception and deceiving to inhabit the same space. Most kids have the same mentality, and people in

[Type here]

general have the same mentality as well. Anyone who is familiar with reverse psychology knows exactly what I mean. Sometimes it is a genuine desire to protect a person when we say don't do something. Other times it's in fact the very way we get them to think about doing something. I wonder how many conversations Adam and Eve had throughout the day in regard to that tree. Their curiosity must have been intense. I can imagine them sitting there looking at it talking to each other asking questions about why God would say don't partake of it. So, there was already a seed of desire planted it only needed to be given attention. They must have had to deal with that feeling of temptation for quite a while. And along Comes the Serpent who is very wise and sees their curiosity and can perceive their temptation. So first they use their eyes to see the tree and were made aware of it and then the serpent uses questions to create a desired effect It was by speaking that the woman was beguiled and manipulated in short deceived. It didn't take too much convincing because we know she only needed a couple of sentences in a short

[Type here]

conversation to be made to ignore the rule given to them by the Lord God. And who was right next to her but Adam.

That was the first example of willing ignorance in our faith and after the deceiver saw how easy it was to manipulate mankind, he was on his way to do as much beguiling as he could. Why? Because in that moment when they both ate his eyes were open as well. He saw how frail human will was. It could be said that he learned the trick of the trade by watching the Lord God create temptation when he told Adam and Eve don't. Then God shows up and asks where is everybody? When Adam and Eve appear the blame game is created. When God asks Adam if he ate of the tree Adam doesn't reply simply yes or no, he points over to the woman and tries to make her accountable for his action (which was doing nothing). This is a good example of how sometimes willing ignorance originates from shame for it is in the denial of something that someone reveals their guilt. But Adam's true fault lay in doing nothing. It is the first example we have of a good man doing nothing in response to evil winning. It seems

[Type here]

man was designed to be deceived and the serpent was meant to deceive. And we know who the serpent was and where he came from and what transpired in heaven previous to the events that transpired on Earth with Adam and eve. PT Barnum once said, "A sucker is born every minute". James Sanborn said, "Deception is everywhere". John Ruskin said, "The essence of lying is in deception not in words". And "All Warfare is based on deception", unknown. That last quote says it all. We are in a war and deception is Lucifer's greatest weapon.

At present we are living in the most controversial of times. It seems chaos is all around us and exists in every aspect of lives from politics to finance to education and even religion. We are in a war and deception is Lucifer's greatest weapon. I am not politically inclined, but I as well as most other Americans, are aghast at the policies enacted by our political leaders. They have created policies which destroy our country from the inside out, the literal definition of corruption. Criminals allowed to walk the streets the same day after being caught

[Type here]

and released even when they are guilty of the crimes. Our borders have been flung open with a reckless abandon and everyone is watching this and trying to understand it. News reports are constantly giving false information and spreading fear and dissension. We are living in a country where our leaders have a policy designed on not only deception but compliance through willing ignorance in order to fit in to the world system. But what does the Bible say about willing ignorance. In Peter 3:5,17 Peter is *warning against forgetting* what they believe as others who knew *but were willingly deceived and forgot*. The ignorance came from forgetting. Forgetting they became ignorant and in so doing opened their hearts and minds to false prophets and to the soul of deception. So how do we guard against spiritual deception? Grow in the word or rather allow the word to grow in you, pray for revelation so you can perceive the essence of a thing or a matter. Do not try to do good but open yourself up to the soul of that which is good and true. Minimize your association with non-believers because you are set apart-be truly holy in that you don't conform to the standard of the world. Give to

[Type here]

be fulfilled and love people, not only in thought but in action. When you walk by people speak, do not be willingly ignorant to their presence. Express to your family and those close to you that you love them as often as possible. Because where God is love is and where love is God is.

Don't distance yourself from your parents, they love you more than you know even if it seems evidence is to the contrary. They would give you the world if they could. Tell your mother and father you love them each night before you go to bed so God's spirit is with you and them in your nightly wanderings. Forgive your parents if they do something which has hurt you. Giving them forgiveness is extending grace and is a way to honor them. Don't get angry at things that are not something you have control over. And things that you do have control over just be aware that your reaction determines the outcome of the dynamic. Be patient with people as well as yourself and give grace to yourself and them that wrong you the way God has given us grace through his love and the love of his son. Learn something new about yourself every day

[Type here]

because awareness to an action leads to knowledge of it and here knowledge is understanding follows and ultimately wisdom comes. Manifest the soul of kindness with your neighbors and strangers because in time of need the people around you will be those who can support you but more than that they are humans brothers and sisters with the same spirit and all striving to achieve growth of the soul; and we all need love and kindness. In other words, open your heart.

Deception is everywhere now, deep fakes, AI and news designed to make people believe what the powers that be want them to believe. This is the information age and yet people are more willing to be ignorant now more than ever, especially in regard to God. Knowledge of Technology does not exalt God in fact the technocrats of this day seek to make themselves into gods using technology. Anytime people aspire to become like God there is a history of bad things happening. It is by the idea that one could become higher than God that the Heavenly War started. There is a saying "a prideful heart before the fall" and this statement has been proven true not

[Type here]

only in scripture from the account of Lucifer and the war in heaven but also in history in regard to people and kingdoms as well. For even though this is the age of information willing ignorance is more widespread now than ever before. One prime example is a movement called woke. The use of the word expresses the essence of willing ignorance. Hypocrisy is an accurate reflection of what these people actually believe. For their belief is centered on waking up to the injustices committed against groups of people and their freedom as well as to have an equality in society by having policies which create not only chaos but division and resentment. For anyone with intelligence the word woke is a reflection and the exemplification of how much pride people take in being willingly ignorant. It is a word that implies rebellion and is that the heart of some of the most deceptive ideals existing today. The mutilation of the soul of the country as reflected in the mutilation of the innocence of our youth is an abomination to the sanctity of our core values as a people. In fact, the so-called trans movement is nothing more than idle worship of the creature known as Baphomet. This kind of behavior has

[Type here]

spread far and wide in an unexplained explosion of political support and educational support. I do not seek to explain the source of darkness and chaos only to point out the possible roots of the tree from which it bears its fruits.

There has been a slow systematic decline which has resulted from intentional implementation of policies which manipulate the very fabric of our society which at one point was based on biblical principles and the idea of freedom in harmony with the structure of a government based on Justice Mercy and fairness. The soul of rebellion against American values is a reflection of the rebellion of Lucifer against God's principles in heaven and this war wages daily. The slow acquiescence to compromise pushes the door of chaos open wider and wider every day. Compromise is Lucifer's primary weapon. It starts with something small, and it continues in a series of yeses until ultimately all core values are gone and there is no line in the sand which to stand in front of and protect. As has been said if you stand for nothing, you'll fall for everything. Our leaders have abandoned us, and our church leaders are more

[Type here]

interested in lining their pockets than teaching or inculcating the soul of Jesus within the body of Christ. There is no accountability in government or educational institutions and each generation is in fact a degeneration of culture and society. To reflect on where all this is coming from and what the driving force behind all this deception and rebellion should be something everyone reflects on every day. There is a kind of material virus that technology engenders within our soul. But where does that come from? It is time we acknowledge that Lucifer is real. He is the boogie man hiding under your bed and he is coming for us all. We are in a battle not only for our own souls but for the soul of our nation. But the good news is if Lucifer is real then so is God and if God is real then so is Jesus which means the Bible is the true word of God. The best way to stop the spread of the virus of willing ignorance is acknowledging the reality of God and his existence. And to return our focus not on doctrine but the virtues taught by our Lord and savior Christ Jesus.

[Type here]

Chapter 3

[Type here]

Hearing and understanding God's message.

In this chapter we will look at the faculty of hearing. One of the most frustrating things to endure is to talk to somebody and repeating the same thing over and over because the person you're talking to doesn't hear you. Why doesn't the person hear you? Are they losing their ability to hear? Maybe they're preoccupied with some other tasks. Or maybe they just aren't interested in what you have to say. In some instances what you have to say is not something they want to hear. When you're talking to somebody maybe they do hear you, but they don't understand, they can hear the words and sounds emanating from your mouth but can't perceive the meaning. This can be caused by not having the ability to process the information transmitted from a language because of a language barrier or insufficient vocabulary, or just a lack of knowledge in regard to the subject being discussed. Perceiving is an insight into information and relation to a

[Type here]

bigger picture. The more knowledge someone has and the more gains understanding of a subject in relation to a bigger picture the more insight or wisdom a person can attain as to how well to use that information to generate new ideas and functions.

But what is information? It is data from senses which is processed as light in the form of signals from words either spoken which are heard or read. The human body is designed very much like a computer which operates off of light and darkness. The nervous routes light to the brain where it congregates and bundles together in a brilliant display of radiance. Much like we as members of the risen Christ gather light and contribute it to the head of our church who is Christ Jesus. The signals are conveyed and transmitted as billions of series of interactions of light. So, we are in fact made of light. The corruption of a soul is the dimming of the light which flows through a person's body hence the term a darkness within. A person who serves the darkness possesses darkness a person who serves light possesses light. It must be noted

[Type here]

here that as Lucifer was known as the light-bringer and deception can be in the form of light as it is today. Technology has engendered a deeper knowledge of the material world and a dimmer and more superficial knowledge of God. For as we know the glory of God makes even the Sun seem dark. So even the light of today's information age nothing compared to God's glory.

The elevation of information and technology is creating the very antithesis of God's wisdom in the form of artificial intelligence. By creating AI and elevating it to godlike status we are worshiping the creation of false light more than the creator. AI makes me think of a famous quote: "I have become death the Destroyers of worlds" Oppenheimer said this at the detonation of the first nuclear bomb, which brought more light to the world as a result of the highest form of technology at that time. It is a frightening realization that Oppenheimer comes to which is why he chose those words to speak at the moment of detonation. For as we see light can destroy and consume in the form of nuclear energy and Fire. But it can also

[Type here]

corrupt in the form of information. The same way the serpent used information from a truth to deceive Adam and Eve.
As we have seen; seeing something can give us some knowledge about it about the information is only visual or appearance based. And deception can easily be accomplished through appearance. In chapter one we have seen it is through not only observation but reflection of a person's or thing's behavior we come to understand its true nature and gain insight into their essence 'soul.

 For modern members of the body of Christ we must rely on building our faculty of hearing as well so we can listen and understand God's message and gain wisdom into the nature of Jesus in order to grow in faith and inculcate his soul in us and among us. In an age of constant bombardment where visual senses are assaulted non-stop by a barrage of visual stimulation it's easy to see (ironically so) why our power of discernment through ocular perception is obscured. It is the impressions we form from data around us which literally program us to behave with the expectation of certain

[Type here]

outcomes based on visual cues that we learn from TV or other sources. Hence the term programming. By associating concepts with images companies can create associations which plant seeds of desired outcomes in our behavior and thinking. Much like Our Lord God did in the Genesis. As previously mentioned, we are actually here to be deceived, this is a fact and it's clearly Illustrated throughout scripture, nit in words but in the behavior illustrated. in Genesis 3: "the woman saw that the tree was good for food and pleasing to the eye". That is the first example of temptation arising from stimulation. It is written plainly for all to see that the eyes are truly the window to the soul. As her desire arose from seeing it so too many of our desires arise from things that we see. As mentioned by associating visual imagery with products and concepts companies can create associations of desire. They can plant seeds of attraction to in order to get an outcome from people. If a company can use visual cues to create a seed of desire to possess, then certainly the same concept applies to Media Outlets in regard to controlling people's thoughts in the events of the world. Everything we read or see in the

[Type here]

media is carefully controlled and distributed by only a handful of people and this is one tentacle of the octopus of deception. But the seed of deception was in fact planted with the tree of knowledge of Good and Evil and it's very planting in the center of the garden by virtue of its proximity equidistant to all areas of the garden, Mo matter where they went the tree was always in plain sight. It was by God's design that man should be deceived for; everywhere the man went in the garden the tree would always be in sight. So, then we can say the association of attraction which led to the temptation of Adam and Eve and the beguiling of them by the serpent was in fact created by Lord God himself simply by the statement "don't".

The Lord God used not only sight but hearing in creating a situation in which both of them could be deceived. The serpent only needed to phrase his statements with a hint of truth mixed with a lie and spoke it aloud. It is the same principle used by the world system which is composed of economic, educational and religious organizations wielding tremendous influence. It is well known that the vast majority

[Type here]

of mainstream media is used to promote agendas to create outcomes. Information is controlled, manipulated and scaled to a level which is beyond imagination. And now media and Technology are working together to create an age of darkness under the guise of information. It is a very prominent example of how light is used to promote darkness. What we see on television and in movies is regulated and censored before it is even delivered via a script to the teleprompter for newscasters to read. Watch the eyes of the news casters very closely and times they look soulless as they read. There is no intelligence in their eyes when they are broadcasting and reading. Consider this carefully, what we see on TV is literally a script being read by someone on TV. By definition they are actors. And actors have the job of making the unreal seem real which is deception. Perhaps this explains the corruption and the level of depravity that exists not only in the television and movie industry but in all other entertainment Industries as well. Journalism in the past was a form of testimony based on the truth of witnesses from an objective standpoint. But over the last 50 years it has degenerated into a form of fact finding that

[Type here]

is twisted to promote a narrative in an effort to deceive viewers and make them believe something. In other words, they take some truth and mix it with lies in order to get people to do what they want. Does that sound familiar to you? The recent Revelations in the last few years on a mass scale of how dishonest and manipulative as well as the depravity not only the news but the entertainment industry as well can be attributed unbridled access to information in this age.

All the information should create more reflection from transparency and leads to revelation; Revelation comes from truth. However as quickly as revelation comes the deceiver tries to create controversy around it by using the truth of that information and take away from its authority. I hope you can see clearly the design of the plan that is unfolding before us from my words. As we know it was not just visual temptation but the hearing of words which finally convinced to eat Eve to act. How powerful is our faculty of hearing. In Romans chapter 10 verse 17 we learned that faith comes from hearing and hearing from the word of God. If faith can come by hearing,

[Type here]

then so too can deception. This is because the fear of the Lord is the beginning of wisdom which comes from understanding which arises fem knowledge. And while this concept is simple, for us to really perceive it from hearing it- we must truly understand the relationship between hearing that Jesus is the word of God and the acknowledgment of God though hearing of the word. Having a direct relationship implied by Romans 10:17 "So then faith cometh by hearing, and hearing by the word of God." That is, faith which is based on hearing about the essence and nature of the soul of Jesus comes from awareness of him which leads to knowledge of him and us and how we relate to him. For none of us today have seen him and so that is why our faith is based on hearing. In John 20:29 Jesus says, "Blessed are they that have not seen and yet have believed." God and our Lord Jesus are so intimately connected because it is by the word that God created the heavens and the Earth. So, any acknowledgment of God will produce knowledge of the word and the knowledge of the word increases understanding of God. Herein lies the mystery of their Oneness and origin of wisdom. We know from studying the New Testament that having ears to hear is a metaphor for

[Type here]

understanding something. In the garden Adam and Eve gained knowledge of the tree from listening to God when he told them "Don't touch that tree". But they did not hear him when he said don't touch that tree. At first it seems like a redundant contradiction but upon further reflection one can see it is not. It is by the application of knowledge one comes to understand its use in a given situation and wisdom arises from the experience of the synergy which results in in the interplay between the two. While much talk has been given to the visual realm of perception let's take a closer look at the auditory realm of perception.

With all the knowledge being poured out through the realm of the visual how much more is being poured out through the realm of the auditory? And how much value does the information from both the Visual and auditory stimulus we receive every day really have to our daily lives? So how do we deal with all the stimulation? We can watch the news and mute the TV and escape the auditory assault on our senses to a degree however we are still subjected to the images. And we

[Type here]

must be aware that even if a person doesn't have the sound on when these news channels or TV shows go to commercials the information is almost completely visually oriented so even if you turn the sound off you are still subjected to the imagery. The imagery is rich and vivid and often times slow motion is used as a way to hypnotize the viewers and engage them unconsciously. One of the best examples I can think of this are the food commercials. The sound on these commercials issues as a kind of subliminal message to supplement the imagery. And within the imagery is contained a lot of data. In many food commercials, (pizza commercials and fast-food commercials come to mind) the background is color oriented and more prominently so by the use of HDTV. These colors are arranged in such a way to create a backdrop against which the imagery of dripping sauces and slowly pulling cheese or slowly falling ingredients is accentuated. All of this combined results in billions of dollars of generated revenue from our consumption that many of us never even consider. We are being fashioned into the image of those who control the world want us to become. They have become as God in their own

[Type here]

minds and have made us from spiritual fruit producers to consumers of the material world in an effort to feed them. The propagation of misinformation extends beyond just food commercials or drink commercials. Many pharmaceutical commercials are advertised by showing people laughing and smiling but towards the end of the commercial there's a laundry list of possible negative side effects that contradicts everything that we're seeing and being presented us within the contents of the commercial. Some of the side effects listed are seriously detrimental to the health of people and can include death and yet people still take these medicines. Those are just two examples of we are being manipulated into willingly ignorant behavior based on deception generated by images on the television. For. at the same time, we're looking at people smiling and laughing we are being told this medicine could do very serious harm Sometimes it's a full 10 seconds of side effects listed which can be almost 20 percent of the commercial.

[Type here]

Television and movies have created an idea of virtual normalcy what we derive from the so-called programming. As mentioned earlier virtual entertainment video entertainment spreads darkness into the soul. How often does the news display anything positive? Almost every night on every broadcast we hear of a flood or a fire or war or some kind of starvation or famine happening. We hear the corruption of our innocent children and the harm done to them. It is increasing daily as if the evil of the world makes no attempt to hide itself. And why should it? We turn a blind eye to it every day. Or, perhaps the evil is in its final throws thrashing and jumping chaotically like a fish out of water gasping for life as it slowly dies. It is running out of time and knows it. It is not political ideology, and it is not cultural. It is literal warfare on the soul of man and the world. The material world is a reflection of the unseen world, Romans 1:20 "For the invisible things of him from the creation of the world are clearly seen, being understood by the things that are made". Eph 6:12 "For we wrestle not against flesh and blood, but against principalities, against powers, against the rulers of the darkness of this
[Type here]

world, against spiritual wickedness in high places". The battle that is occurring on Earth is a reflection of the battle that is occurring in the heavenly realm.

I don't know where we are in relation to what many consider end times prophecy. And though scripture clearly mentions the climate in which the return of Our Lord Jesus will return, it could apply to any age. There are always wars there are always wars and rumors of wars there are always famines and plagues and there have always been false prophets. But what separates our age from previous ages is not only the increase in propagation of known darkness and the spread of willing ignorance but the awareness of it as well. At no other time in history has man been able to access data and be aware of almost everything happening on a scale that exists today. Something to think about.

The internet has become a substitute source of knowledge that we gain truth from instead of the soul of God. For we have abandoned the awareness of God and there is no fear of God and without fear of God there can be no beginning of

[Type here]

wisdom without the beginning of wisdom deception is easily propagated and the deceiver can continue to control the world and the souls of those who in habitat of it. There is a reason why all these things are coming together as they are. It is like a puzzle to being put together to reveal the totality of a picture.

The knowledge of something creates an opportunity to understand it and understanding opens the door to wisdom. as doves. as the nature of Lucifer is to deceive and he deceives by mixing lies with truth.

As it is written in Matthew 10: 6 "Behold, I send you forth as sheep in the midst of wolves: be ye therefore wise as serpents, and harmless as doves". So the point of this is having the awareness that he is real is to gain knowledge and understanding of deception and how it is manifested on a daily basis. I don't know if there are any people here who can truly change the world, but we can each change our own personal environment. The more of these pockets of positivity and the more believers of Christ assemble together the more

[Type here]

can spread and the larger the body of Christ grows. These pockets of positive energy and love will continue to manifest and spread creating a gigantic nerves system which can grow into one body of light in preparation for our head to join together with.   For only when the body is joined can it have a head to lead it. To clarify in no uncertain terms what I mean is if we want to see the return of Jesus, we must make a way for him. He is waiting for us. we must ask him to return not in some desperate call for help or plea of emotional outcry. But in a tone of sincere desire asking our Lord "will you come to take your place"? asking Our Father "Will you please send our Lord God and brother to us"? Too often prayer is something that people apply as a function of asking but not really asking directly with an attitude of childlike devotion. Most people pray more out of expectation to have something done for us. But in the Lord's prayer the words "thy will be done" clearly mean we should be asking for the God's will to be done, not our own. Most of us know that the word pray means to ask, but that doesn't mean to actually use the word "pray" when we are in prayer. It's a kind vocalization based on repetition,

[Type here]

for example "Lord, I pray you, Lord gives me or them, Lord help me or him or her. Lord, I need" etc. If you take the time and reflect about how most people pray it isn't asking. It's more of an assumption based on expectation. through speaking. But that isn't how we can connect in communion with God. It will take some getting used to but phrasing your need or want or the desire to help someone or to ask for something for someone else should be phrased in a way like you're asking someone close to you to help you. And always with remembrance that if its God's will then it should be done. Saying "please Lord" before you pray does not open a channel of direct communication. I am not an authority on how to pray but if we want to establish an intimate relationship with God then we need to reflect on how we speak to him when we are alone with him, or when we think about what we want to ask for.

    Up to this point we've discussed the news and TV but what about music? How does that impact our sense of hearing God's message for us? And by extension our capacity to understand. There are many outlets that people can plug into

[Type here]

for enjoyment or entertainment. Among those is music. It should be obvious here music can affect us because it is entirely auditory. And since it has been demonstrated that frequencies have a distinct effect which is profound on cell structures and plants it follows it can affect the very arrangement of our molecular makeup. I remember the days of bands like Motley Crue and Metallica and AC/DC. The so-called hard rock. The long hair, the ripped jeans, the attitude of "smokin in the boy's room". Even early rap when it produced an increase in gold and jewelry sales.

People who listen to certain music have certain attitudes and dressed in a way which reflects the "style" of that music. Where others say I style I use soul. When people hear music the hearing of it affected their minds in a way which fills their lives. Their lives and habits and how they think and related to people. Music today and the soul it creates can be contrasted to the music of the '60s and seventies and there was a world of difference, literally. The evidence of the change in the soul of music and how it has created a change in the soul of our

[Type here]

country can be palpably observed. To be clear I am not advocating that people stop listening to music all together. I don't listen to music and avoid watching the programming which creates a toxic mental atmosphere spewed out on television, I do watch shows on Netflix and Amazon Prime, but I choose selectively. I think most people do the same thing. The main reason I choose these kinds of being platforms is because in the past they had no commercials but nowadays however the commercials have become an all-pervasive intrusion into our entertainment. Advertisement has penetrated all platforms of entertainment and it is becoming more of the body of the program than the entertainment itself. It may seem like a boring life without music but if you are constantly listening to something then how can you hear God's message? If a person were to hear God's message for them, it would change their idea of how they value silence. I suggest turning off the radio in your car and learn what silence can offer you by giving yourself a chance to literally unplug from emotional influences when you can. Listening is a skill that must be practiced. People spend their day in a flood of

[Type here]

noise and drown themselves in it. I propose finding an island of silence where you can create a beach for the serenity of your soul and tune in. For those who wish to draw close to God I remind you of Elijah and his experience in Kings 1:13 "And, behold, the LORD passed by, and a great and strong wind rent the mountains, and brake in pieces the rocks before the LORD; but the LORD was not in the wind: and after the wind an earthquake; but the LORD was not in the earthquake: and after the earthquake a

fire; but the LORD was not in the fire: and after the fire a still small voice. and it was so, when Elijah heard it, "Psalm 46:10" Be still, and know that I am God". If you want to have a relationship with God, you must be able to be silent. Not only be silent but be in silence. For the passive form of "I am" is "to be" so if you want to experience the feeling of "I am" you must be. Listening to music transports us to another kind of existence where we are not concerned with the affairs of the world or anything around us.

[Type here]

When we listen to music we are absorbed in the lyrics as well as the music itself and we allow ourselves to be overcome with something that can distract us from the troubles of the world. But If you want to talk to someone and there is a lot of noise, what do you do? Try to create a more silent atmosphere. In fact, when people are having a conversation and its too loud often people will say "let's go someplace quieter where we can talk".

God is saying that to all of us every day. You have the awareness, the knowledge of God through all the evidence around you and in that silence and knowledge of his power you will come to understand his soul which is in all of us. You will come to understand the depths of his being spirit which is in all of us. Create a more conscious awareness of how your soul is connected to your body by his spirit. From that understanding wisdom can grow and fill your mind. I can assure you that achieving true communion with the spirit of God will fill you with more inner peace and the radiance of his voice is greater than any musical instrument or song. It feels

[Type here]

like a giant deep within you in the center of your being that is yelling into a megaphone and at the same time standing over you and speaking loudly with a voice that comes inside and outside of you at the same time. It is frightening, delightful and it will reverberate through every molecule of your being. It is not a voice in your head, it is not the "voice of conscience" it is not a feeling or intuition. It is a literal voice.

Another example of how visual and auditory influences affect us through our soul realm is through the of the emergence of the hip hop and Pop culture phenomenon. My intention of what I am about to say in the following paragraphs is not to insult or berate or take away from the value that people perceive about that genre. In fact, there are some people in that genre who represent themselves in the entirety of the truth of who they are as artists, and this is the reason they are successful. However, the majority of the industry is made up actors who promote sex, drugs, violence the worship of money and wealth and a general attitude of rebellion against authority in general. And while some of the

[Type here]

performers claim to believe in God and say what they rap about or sing about or how they dress and what they do in their videos is just an act Its a contradiction. because anyone who lives a life based on goodness would not engage in a performance of deception. Even if what they are doing is an "act" it's based on the intent to project an image which engenders a kind of behavior which is corrosive.

Most often times the lyrics are about anything materialistic that would give the appearance of a level of wealth which is to be desired. And it also promotes status and the idea of "street Credit" through violent acts which give the person an aura of power. In a word it is worship of the exaltation of the self. The style of clothing and "fashion? Is the soul of slothfulness and an arrogance of not caring which screams willful ignorance. With the advent of this form of entertainment there has been a spread of rebellion, violence, drug use and overall lack of care in regard to those around people. It is an embodiment of what it means to be willingly ignorant, and it has corrupted the youth and consciousness of

[Type here]

our country. There are teenage boys and girls walking around wearing clothes that are falling of their body and literally walking around showing the world their ass.

This is a statement of rebellion and while most of them dress this way to imitate, they are actually bending to envy and worshipping idols. They don't understand what kind of damage it does to them because they have no leaders to look up to by comparison. This is not a fault of the industry itself but of the policy makers which have sold their souls and allowed these different forms of deception to penetrate the minds of the youth and it corrupts their hearts. Young people imitate what they see others who they think are successful in life do and so they are easily influenced to behave not just when listening to the music but after the music is over. It is a kind of disharmony which disrupts the molecular level of their being.

In describing sound and hearing I am reminded of a movie I saw many years ago called "What the bleep do we know"? In the movie they showed experiments done by a Japanese

[Type here]

scientist Dr Masaru Emoto, This experiment involved different bottles of water and different ranges of emotions and sounds that were projected verbally by different people and sound waves into the bottles of water. Dr. Emoto was demonstrating the effects of sound and resonance on consciousness The bottles were then allowed to sit for a period of time and after the bottles sat for a period of time, they were analyzed on a molecular level to see what if any the emotional vibrations had on their molecular structure. There are as many articles disputing the reports of his findings as there are refuting so I can only this; plants respond to music, people respond to music, directed energy weapons affect people through resonance. Glass can be shattered with certain musical resonances. So according to all these different verifiable, real world everyday examples I would tend to believe it. Why is it when we go into a church or a temple there is a peacefulness and calm to the environment? And when people listen to music there is clearly an effect on them. I offer an opportunity to the reader to use Google to search that movie and see the results for yourself.

[Type here]

Because we do know that what people say can hurt us or help us, as we know "faith comes through hearing? Emotions do affect the molecular structure of water and since the human body is made mostly of water; Gen 2:7 *"But there went up a mist from the earth and watered the whole face of the ground*. And the LORD God formed man of the dust of the ground and breathed into his nostrils the breath of life; and man became a living soul". We know that we are formed with mostly water. So, frequencies affect our bodies in different ways according the form of vibrations. The old saying "sticks and stones may break my bones, but words will never hurt". Is something that we need to think about very carefully. But more than that it illustrates just how deleterious the effect of aggressive or loud or music that contains violent intentions inherent to the lyrics can be on a person's soul. I don't mean to say that hip-hop is solely to blame for the degeneration of our culture and the decline of the last two generations, but it is a tool which the force of evil uses. Before hip hop there was rap and all its various forms. There is even

[Type here]

Christian rap which seldom does well or sells because it isn't a part mainstream culture. As we know; sex sells, violence sells and anything that is associated with the mainstream popular cult sells. We have been guided into a way of thinking and living that only benefits the growth of things that harm us. The spread of darkness is like a fungus which is growing out of control and needs to be sterilized. And as the saying goes: "Sunshine is the best disinfectant".

The ears as organs of perceptions are designed to increase our ability to gain wisdom. Like all our senses. Our eyes are the same. Our senses of feel and smell and taste all have the same function of helping us to draw closer to God. Much could be said about our sense of feeling as being manipulated through different fabrics and materials and textures in foods as well as drinks and just food in general. All the sensual things that feeling brings with it are exploited first through our sense of sight which brings a desire to draw nearer to an object so we can gain a more direct experience of it, just like in Genesis 3:6 "And when the *women saw that the tree was good for food and that it was pleasant to the eyes* and a tree to be desired to

[Type here]

make one wise, she took of the fruit thereof". And drugs exploit human senses to a degree that sems other worldly at times. There is a drug for any kind of stimulation that a person could want to feel. Street drugs are everywhere, and they are used by a variety if people for all kinds of things.

There are also medical drugs which are promoted by the medical industry for depression, attention deficit disorder, bipolar disorder (and there are a few kinds of that), obsessive compulsive behavior, and the list goes on. Every couple of years a new "disorder "comes out and then the industry gets a boost in sales because of the "awareness" that is raised to that newly discovered "disease". The sense of feeling has been manipulated not only externally but internally as well. As we have seen, internal feelings are easily manipulated and if a person takes enough of something it will affect their DNA, so some effect can be passed on to children.

The more medicine that is produced the more problems are produced. I support the need to treat someone if they truly have a mental problem or disorder. But the way children are

[Type here]

spoon-fed medicine it is no wonder they have so many problems after they become adults. Every one of the five senses and their relationship to gaining knowledge and wisdom and how they are used to manipulate us and deceive us. Just as constantly being bombarded with visual stimulation blinds us and secular music drowns our hearing a flood of noise and drugs and medicines cloud our minds and pollute our ability to discern so too does our sense of taste get used to deceive us.

  The addition of flavorings and additives to all our food and beverages is no different than the way TVs and computers and cell phones are "upgraded" frequently to enhance our "user experience". The expression "enhance user experience" should be followed by "so we can drag you more into the virtual world and consume more of your soul through the manipulation of your sensory organs daily. "

  I have noticed in the last couple of years many consumables taste different. Things I ate when I was younger tasted very different today. And I don't mean to imply my tastes have

[Type here]

changed, I mean, the food itself tastes strange. I have asked several people if they have noticed it too and most concur. If you go to Starbucks and watch them, make the coffee drinks you can see the people who work there pumping flavored syrup into the different drinks to add flavors. I cannot understand how someone can do that and then consume it. It is at best, flavored corn syrup. I don't even know if it's corn syrup, but the flavoring is something made in a lab with chemicals that must have some effect on our chemistry.

And that's just one example, all the "flavoring" of food extends to all items. When you eat a chocolate cake do you think its chocolate you are eating? This question may sound like something out of the Matrix movie, when Morpheus and Neo are fighting and Morpheus asks, "you think that's air your breathing?" Nowadays, I don't know what we are breathing.

Everything we buy, see or read is most likely is not real. Things are real in the sense that they exist and we can see and touch them, but not real in the sense of not being what we are told they are. It is part of the deception. There is a lot debate

[Type here]

on whether we are living in a simulation and reality not being real. In a way this is a simulation, because we create our own realities through the choices we make. And eventually one or way another, the plug will be pulled. These statements are not intended to create despair or a sense of doom and gloom. Just as with acknowledging God's existence which leads to a knowledge of and understanding of his plan for us, before we can overcome the deceiver, we must first acknowledge his reality and his design. After acknowledging it we can understand it and learn how to overcome it.

   The horror of the fast-food industry is an industry that needs no in-depth introduction or discussion to understand how they are temples of gluttony and greed as well as indulgence. There have been movies such as Supersize me which clearly show the effects of what happens to the human body if it is subjected to fast food on a frequent basis. And there were many news reports about the pink slime that a certain fast-food chain uses for their hamburger "meat" online and on several news channels

[Type here]

Food is an Achilles heel for everyone, and it takes discipline to keep your diet from becoming something that enslaves you to it. But there is something that most people don't stop to consider and that is the people that work at the fast-food restaurants. The character of people that work of these restaurants can range in extreme degrees of temperament and capability as well as ages. One thing which usually happens at those kinds of places is the complacency and attitude of not caring much about the production of the food, just" get it out". because the goal of fast food is, convenience the food is made with little to no care and is subjected to the handling of many different people throughout the process of being prepare and given to you. Whatever negativity the people are feeling goes into that food and you eat it. Reflect on that.

You are not just eating the product; you are consuming the energy of everything involved in the chain of events in that process from beginning to end. There is a reason why things are hallah and kosher. And that is another reason for praying

[Type here]

over our food. It might seem irrelevant to many people but everything in life is based on a frequency. If there were no need for something, then we wouldn't have a precedent for it and after a precedent is established a tradition is created. So, there is a reason for making food kosher.

The processing of making food Kosher back to the Old testament and it was a commandment given to the Israelites to make their food "spiritually clean". The three basic rules that are observed today are the animals must be land animals with a spit hoof and only get their nutrition from eating grass. Seafood must have fins and scales no shellfish and Meat and dairy cannot be eaten together. But within the process of preparing the animals at slaughter there are more rules such as diluting the meat in hot water and salt to get the blood out. Today, most people will say its just done out of a tradition and that is true, but it also serves a purpose of cleansing the food before you eat it.

Another aspect of our sense of taste is that after you eat something that "tastes good" you will always have an appetite

[Type here]

for it. After eating at McDonald's hamburgers kids seldom want a hamburger from home, or after a restaurant pizza when you eat a pizza from a grocery store which you cook in your oven it's just not the same. After we are seduced by a greater stimulus than we are accustomed to any stimulus that doesn't match that frequency can't compare and we have a new threshold. Addiction starts with a behavior which introduces a chemical that helped the brain release more of a certain chemical than what is is accustomed to and because its exogenous our own body stops producing the same chemical and slowly we have to rely more and more on that outside stimulus to provide the release of that chemical which our body would normally make in a given quantity on its own. After drinking soft drinks its difficult for most people to just be satisfied with water because the caffeine and sugar provide a stimulus to our senses that water can't. Often what we want supersedes what we need, and that is a slippery slope to embark on. But the information which we are blinded by constantly tell us we need this or we need that to be happy or to fit in or to be accepted. We continue to be deceived every

[Type here]

day according to our senses and the data they collect. Most of us do it to ourselves, Lucifer just gives us the tools and the thought of trying it.

So how do we win this struggle? We must remember. 1John1;1-4,"That which was formed from the beginning, which we have heard, which we have seen with our eyes, we looked upon and have touched with our hands concerning the word of life-the life was made manifest, and we have seen it, and testify to it and proclaim to you eternal life, which was with the Father and was made manifest to us-that which we have seen and heard we proclaim also to you, so that you too may have fellowship with us; and indeed our fellowship is with the Father and with his Son Jesus Christ. And we are writing these things so that our joy may be complete". Use your senses to glorify God and he will draw near to you. It sounds like it's too good to be true but it is not and it is a personal journey to embark on and discover the treasures that await you.   The daily deterioration of our senses contributes to the eroding away of the fabric of morality and of God's spirit here on

[Type here]

earth. To be clear when I say God's spirit, I literally mean breath. For it is by breath we have life Gen 2;7" And the Lord God formed man of the dust of the ground and breathed into his nostrils the <u>breath of life;</u> and man became a living soul". I am always drawn to the words "living soul" as if that denotes another kind of soul which could exist.

  It is interesting that there is no air outside of our atmosphere the only way we can live naturally is if we are here on Earth. That means that all life comes from the Breath of God. Anything that gives the Breath of God or can attribute its life to the Breath of God is of the spirit of God. Trees take in toxins that are harmful to humans and convert it to the toxins to air which is necessary so we can breathe and have life. The destruction of the rain forests and natural habitats, (as well as the oceans and sky) and the rapid industrialization of man is literally destroying the Spirit of God. Can you see the reality of this? And as we are endowed with a soul which is connected to our bodies by the Spirit of God in the form of breathe the physical destruction of the Spirit of God which permeates the

[Type here]

Earth, is reflected in the destruction of man's Soul through the fabrication of tools of deception which attack our sense organs and impact our ability to perceive God through these sense organs in our soul.

Reread Genesis chapter 2 verse 7 and you will see a distinct and clear delineation of spirit and soul. Hebrews 4:12 "For the word of God is quick, and powerful, and sharper than any two-edged sword, <u>piercing even to the dividing asunder of soul and spirit</u> ". Often we use the terms interchangeably but they are used to describe specific and distinct parts of how we were formed and what our existence is based on. In fact, for anyone who asks for proof of God's existence I would suggest taking a deep breath and realize that God is always with you, in you and through you. As God is Love and the Spirit of God is his breath, every time you breath you are filling yourself with the love of God. Perhaps we should consider John 4:24 "God is a Spirit: and they that worship him must worship him in spirit and in truth". And John 1:4 "Beloved, let us love one another: for love is of God; and everyone that loveth is born of God, and

[Type here]

knoweth God. He that loveth not knoweth not God; for God is love."

While all life has a seed of a soul not all life will grow that seed into the perfect knowledge of God. All animals have a soul but they can't achieve a more perfect knowledge of God. As it is said, many are called but few are chosen, Matthew 22:14 "For many are called but few are chosen". To be a living soul means we can continually grow our souls and not just possess a soul. And all beings have the capability to grow their souls, not just people. Have you ever seen a dog and thought, thatch a smart dog? Anything with soul has the capacity to learn so that they may grow their souls. What separates animals form mankind is we can come to a fuller understanding of God and so we have been given dominion over them from the beginning. Gen 1;28 "And God blessed them, and God said unto them, be fruitful, and multiply, and replenish the earth, and subdue it: and have dominion over the fish of the sea, and over the fowl of the air, and over every living thing that moveth upon the earth". We have a capacity

[Type here]

to increase intelligence so that our soul can grow in the knowledge of God in preparation to receive our Lord Jesus when he returns.

[Type here]

[Type here]

Chapter 4

The Genesis account viewed through a

different lens.

At the close of the last chapter, we took a glimpse at how the impact of just one sentence in Genesis 1:7 can impact the entire view of how we understand scripture can affect our entire view. The difference in function between soul and spirit changes the idea of what the "holy spirit" is. If all life and spirit come from God, it is already Holy. So how can we be filled with the holy spirit again if we were already born with it? As we know the word holy just means set apart for a religious or a specific purpose. So what people are implying when they use the term holy spirit is more properly, the Holy Soul". Through

[Type here]

God's spirit we are already set apart from them and we are made a little lower,

Psalms 8:4 "What is man that you are mindful of him, And the Son of man that You visit him". We can see that we have been set apart from the angels. And because the angles cant die they don't need breathe and by virtue of this fact they are not in need of bodies but they are possibly souls, (authors opinion). What makes a little lower is we can experience death. I don't say die because that implies some finality but when we experience death it is only a sleep. Daniel 12:2 "And many of them that sleep in the dust shall awake, some to everlasting life and some to shame and everlasting contempt." And we know also what we have been set apart from is in fact the world system. Romans 12:2 "And be not conformed to the image of this world".

[Type here]

I propose that it is not a new breath or spirit which fills us but the Holy soul, which Jesus poured out into the world at his death that dwells in us from the realization that we already possess the spirit of God through acknowledging him and his son and the understanding of the germ of radiance our souls possess which is fertilized by the joining of our souls to the soul of Our Lord Christ Jesus. It is not something which causes us to start speaking gibberish or makes us into some magical force which can make a blind person see. Or grow an arm for an amputee. It is receiving access to the soul of Jesus. He came not to create some new form of breath but to release a way for our souls to join to his soul through the spirit given to us by God. He came to enliven our souls. I understand this will not sit well with many readers. But we often see passages and skim over them with no second thought and no reflection. For example, Psalms 62:1 "Find rest, O my soul, in God alone" , he doesn't say

[Type here]

find rest my spirit, he says soul. Again, in Psalms 63:1 "O God, my soul thirsts for you." Mathew 16:26 "For what is a man profited, if he shall gain the whole world, and lose his own soul? Or what shall a man give in exchange for his soul."

 When Jesus was in the wilderness and Lucifer came to tempt him, he refused him because it was his soul that Lucifer wanted not his spirit. If Jesus gave in to temptation his soul would no longer be his to give. And we would not have redemption or access to regeneration of our souls. How many people are running around talking about the holy ghost already? Most of us equate a soul with a ghost. So, people are already saying Holy Soul, but they are confusing it with spirit. This is not a matter of semantics, and the distinction should be made every time a person opens their mouth between the spirit of God and Holy Soul. This is not a matter of opinion as it clearly references the distinction not only in genesis but in many

[Type here]

other parts of scripture. And we don't read God is a soul and must be worshipped as a soul.

So, there is a reason why those words are clearly delineated. As already discussed, consciousness is generated from our soul which is joined to our body by the spirit or breathe of God. There is a plethora of confusion surrounding these terms.

Not only Aramaic, Hebrew and Greek but also Latin has played a role in the evolution of the Bible which we use today.The Bible was written in such a way to be translated later into a language which would articulate specifically the ideas we were meant to understand according to our modern-day language. That is why solely relying on linguistics to add understanding to what is already there often yields so much confusion to these words and lends itself to so many ways we can derive meaning. There times when it can give insight. But The Bible is the living

[Type here]

word. It is the soul of God. In Deuteronomy 4:2 we read "you shall not add to the word which I command you nor take away from it" In revelations 22:18-19 "If anyone adds to these things God will add to him the plagues that are written in this book". Adding something doesn't have to mean adding words to a specific sentence and by contrast it *could* mean trying to use old languages to interpret it as it has been translated after it already evolved into the language it was meant to be in for a specific age. The language for the general understanding from which it could be disseminated to rest of the world seems (in my opinion} to be English. While Spanish and Mandarin are the two most widely spoken languages in the world, (Mandarin because of the Chinese population) we don't see scripture being translated into English from Chinese or Spanish as the source. They are translated *from English* into those languages. And it is the same all over the world. I have not researched how many countries use the

[Type here]

Hebrew or Greek scrolls to use as versions from which to translate directly into their native languages, but I would bet it's not many.

So, the understanding of Genesis from a new perspective begins with a realization of the knowledge that spirit and soul are two distinct things.

Acts 17:28 "For in him we live, and move, and have our being". This agrees fully with God being in and through *all things* living have life and how humans live and breathe and have their being in God. John 6:63 "the words I speak to you, they are spirit, and they are life".

That was a very circuitous way to arrive back to a point where we can continue with the content of this chapter, but a necessary understanding must be established. As discussed in the previous chapter the roles of not only Lucifer as the serpent and deceiver but humans as the deceived are clearly defined. One is to be the deceiver

[Type here]

and one is to be deceived through the carnal nature of willing ignorance.

From the verses of Genesis 3:12 and 13 we see that both Adam and Eve shifted the blame when questioned from themselves to someone else. One of the effects of willing ignorance aside from easily being deceived is the lack of accountability for one's actions. Nobody who is willingly ignorant will admit fault or accept responsibility for something they do or take part in. To be willingly ignorant is ignoring your participation in an action because of the fear of it being known and the shame associated with it. And the early part of Genesis Adam and Eve have no shame because they had done nothing wrong up to that point, but an immediate effect of the action was shame. Or rather an acknowledgment of shame and by extension the realization in humanity of Shame. The shifting of blame to avoid shame is a key indicator of willing ignorance. When someone denies that they have

[Type here]

done something if they have truly not done it, they will not be ashamed or feel conviction from their conscience and have guilt. But what does the Genesis account have to do with how we been living in war between a deception and truth for the last two thousand years? In Genesis 2: 15 it sates the beginning of our war started at the point of when Eve and Adam took of the fruit. I should clarify the distinction between the war in heaven our war on Earth. We are just soldiers on a battlefield. In Revelation 12:7 we learn where the battle started "And there was war in heaven: Michael and his angels fought against the dragon; and the dragon fought and his angels" continuing on "And the great dragon was cast out, that old serpent, called the Devil, and Satan, which deceiveth the whole world: he was cast out into the earth, and his angels were cast out with him". As we see the real war started in heaven and it came to Earth after God made us. Please pay attention to the two names given to Lucifer. Those two names are used to describe his functions on Earth.

[Type here]

And his role as deceiver is clearly defined. To understand why this event is important we must look at the creation account in Genesis 1. But before we dive into this, I want to emphasize the precision and detail which is throughout the Bible. Simply looking at how specific and how much attention to detail is given in Leviticus Numbers and Deuteronomy as well as every other book in scripture we know that everything in scripture is written for a specific reason and every word use is used on with a particular purpose The book is not written in a haphazard fashion where the authors go back and forth as if forgetting something to find a previous mention of and referencing it. In other words, there's no rehashing for clarification of the author for the reader. It is also important to understand that anything dealing with reported history, or any world system or institution related to the word whether it be education or science and history has been subjected scholarly uncertainty since the beginning of

[Type here]

society's journey down the path to truth. I don't need to point out as an example of how the education system has been under scrutiny about what is being taught at primary schools and Pre-K and kindergartens to children. They are being taught to question their own biology and are being taught that homosexuality is OK, as well as the idea that they could be some other gender than what they were born as is being pushed onto children under the guise of teaching tolerance and acceptance.

Tolerance and acceptance here mean compromise. The events which have taken place in children's education in the last decade or so and particularly in the last few years is truly unbelievable. It is a stark indication of the evil and the chaos of the systems of the world and how they are losing control of their narrative. It has been spreading unfettered for hundreds of years but now people are beginning to wake up to the deception. Corruption of innocence is a crowing jewel in the diadem of evil.

[Type here]

Colleges have been hiring based on DEI programs as well as other careers and industrial offices in conjunction with governmental standard. People are being hired not based on the qualifications and the accreditation in relation to their level of professionalism and training but only on the basis of their skin color or ethnic background. We have seen the disastrous results of this program and how it has affected almost every industry and standard in the country. One only needs to look at the crime statistics, the suicide rates and a drastic decline in educational standards to validate the ideas that have been discussed here and the ramifications these implications have on the sole of our nation. And not only on the soul of our nation but on the psyche of our nation. It is truly ironic that anyone who challenges these policies are labeled as a racist or intolerant Nazi or anti-American. While they yell and talk about the principles of tolerance and acceptance, they become willingly ignorant to the views of others and

[Type here]

are hypocritical in the way they ignore and accuse people who disagree with them as being wrong ultimately violating their own principles which they claim to support. They in essence become a kind of Satan which is the Hebrew word for accuser. So essentially, they are literally embodying the consciousness of Satan. In a free Society everyone is to choose what they believe and think. How we want is according to our own beliefs, but an acknowledgment must also be made that we must maintain the accountability of what we say and do. Not having accountability or acting out of self-interest or profit when you know it can willingly harm others or engage in behavior that willingly harms others abuses the right of freedom. And if these people enacting these policies and following these policies and engaging these policies truly don't know what they are doing then they lack awareness to even the most basic fundamental principles and intelligence of American society. They also

[Type here]

lack a basic understanding about the difference between constructive and destructive decisions and behavior. How could they have been put into positions of authority unless it was under the authority of willing ignorance itself. Which is not of God and goodness but darkness. There is clearly a dark force behind all these the strange and absurd policies, and it is guiding our nation's leaders. So with the knowledge of how dark and manipulated our world institutions are we return to Genesis 1 and 2. I would like to draw attention to Genesis 1: 26."And God said, Let us make man in our image, after our likeness: and let them have dominion over the fish of the sea, and over the fowl of the air, and over the cattle, and over all the earth, and over every creeping thing that creepeth upon the earth". If we analyze this, we have some interesting words used. God is working with an associate or associates in creating man in their image after their likeness. Genesis 2: 6 says "And God blessed them, and God said unto them, Be fruitful,

[Type here]

and multiply, and replenish the earth, and subdue it: and have dominion over the fish of the sea, and over the fowl of the air, and over every living thing that moveth upon the earth". What is the imperatives God gives them? Be fruitful, multiply, replenish. Many people don't notice that it distinguishes here between being fruitful as well as multiplying. They are clearly two distinct things. It also says to replenish. The word replenish implies doing something again. So why would God tell them to replenish the Earth if there wasn't some previous iteration of mankind? And lastly, they are to have dominion. To subdue every living creature. But there are no rules telling them not to do anything or laws to govern a moralistic aspect of their behavior. Why is this worded so specifically? And in Genesis 29 he says "And God said, Behold, I have given you every herb bearing seed, which is upon the face of all the earth, and every tree, in the which is the fruit of a tree yielding seed; to you it shall be for meat" This is in stark contrast to the words written in Genesis 2:7 . God specifically told them to eat anything they wanted from the garden and saw

[Type here]

everything as good. In fact, everything was not just good but very good. At this point there was only a couple of commands multiply, be fruitful, dominion and eat whatever you want. At this point there isn't even any detail into how God that form of humans. To reiterate, there is no command does not touch or not eat or not do anything. In fact, these beings had no law and didn't need any law. They were simply being and multiplying. The be fruitful aspect is another subject altogether and I will save that for another book. Some scholars will say the sentence be fruitful and multiply was a conjoined phrase because of the expression of "and" so it expresses multiply is used to denote a result of being fruitful. But if God wanted that to be illustrated it would have been worded in way which clearly states that multiplying was a function of being fruitful. Their logic is like saying getting get married and have babies is the same thing. Getting married is a distinct act from having babies. So, this is a

[Type here]

subject that requires more attention than is suitable for this chapter.

 The next chapter of Genesis we start with everything being finished and complete. Genesis 2:1Thus the heavens and the earth were finished, and all the host of them and God resting. And. Genesis: 3 "And God blessed the seventh day and sanctified it: because that in it **he** had rested from all his work which God created and made". So, while there was a singular being at work in the process of everything before his creation of man, there was plurality of beings implied at work in the making of man. Does that mean the other beings or other being was still at work doing something? Genesis 2: 4 curiously starts out with an apparently new account of the generations of the heavens- plural and of the earth and the day the Lord God made the earth and the heavens. "These are the generations of the heavens and of the earth when they were created, in the day that the Lord God made the earth and the heavens", This is the

[Type here]

Lord God and not one God or more than one God at work. This contrasts with God (singular) creating light and separating it from darkness and creating the totality of insistence in Genesis 1. Genesis 2 is introducing a transition a handing over of the power structure and the process of creation. We have different description of events with no days only the generation of elements. And then it says the Lord God began his work. The function of things not being generated and things not happening is used instead of things happening, for example. Genesis 2:5 "And every plant of the field before it was in the Earth and every herb before it grew." The Lord God had not caused it to rain upon the Earth and there was not a man to till the ground". That is quite a transition. And there must be a reason for it. Perhaps in the next sentence there is a clue. Genesis 2:6 "But there went up a mist from the ground and watered the hole face of the Earth". The primary element of which we are composed of is

[Type here]

introduced. Immediately following that chapter, we see what other element man is formed by. Genesis 2:7 "And the Lord God formed man of the dust of the ground and breathed into his nostrils the breath of life; and man became a living soul". It is very important to realize that all things in this creation are about the garden of Eden specifically, not the earth itself. Genesis 2:8 "And the LORD God planted a garden eastward in Eden; and there he put the man whom **he** had formed.

And out of the ground made the LORD God to grow every tree that is pleasant to tonight, and good for food; the tree of life also in the midst of the garden, and the tree of knowledge of good and evil." So not only is the purpose of man as being described clearly in Genesis 2:5 "and there was not a man to till the ground". completely different in Genesis 1:26, but he was completely alone. And as we read his only purpose was to till the ground. So, this Lord God created a place specifically for things to grow not on the Earth but in one location of the Earth Slop for a moment and reflect on these words. This

[Type here]

is an entirely different set of circumstances with much more details about one particular place on the Earth and an entity new being and entirely new set of rules and ordinances in a different place. In the creation of man in Genesis 1:26 there is no mention of where that being gets

is spirit and there is no mention of a soul, much less a living soul. But let's imagine if there is a son and he sees his father do something, is it possible that he himself would attempt to do it better in order to make his father proud? John 5:17 "But Jesus answered them, My Father worketh hitherto, and I work. Then Jesus and said unto them, Verily, verily, I say unto you, The Son can do nothing of himself, but what he seeth the Father do: for what things soever he doeth, these also doeth the Son likewise. For the father loveth the son, and sheweth him all things that himself doeth: and he will shew him greater works than these, that ye may marvel". That is in response to the pharisees that were questioning him about him equal with God. Apparently, he is using an example of a precedent. We already know the

[Type here]

detail and precision with which all the first five books as well as the entirety of the Bible is written. It follows that the argument of Genesis 2 being a recap of chapter one as if the author wanted to revisit creation as if he had forgotten some intimate details and decided to go back and clarify. This just doesn't seem likely. It would be like me telling you a story and then forgetting something and then having to go back and add some details because I forgot. I doubt the intelligence of the author of The Pentateuch or the first five books of the Bible had the mindset of forgetting to add something after he wrote it considering the details and the specifications that are included in the history account of Exodus and the measurements and numbers of the other three books of the Pentateuch. There are some who suggest that the god in Genesis 1 is an aspect of our God, and the God of Genesis 2 is a different aspect. The use the samples of Elohim and El as used in Hebrew to denote different

[Type here]

aspects along with YHWH. But if the word is living and if Jesus is the word of God who has been resurrected and whose soul has been infused into all life on the planet and if everything in the bible points to his being and his standing in the Glory of God. We must acknowledge that if the Bible is the living word of God then it is connected to the soul of Our Lord Jesus., Which means as we grow in Christ so does the nature of our consciousness of the written word in which was made flesh/ And as we are members of the soul of Christ the understanding of the word grows in proportion to our soul as we continue to grow in Christ. I mean to say the Bible is the literal message of the word of Our Lord to us. It is alive, it is not just some book.

Plainly speaking-It just seems outright ignorant to look at these two chapters and not consider or give thought to their being any reason to these two accounts being different simply because the author decided to go back

[Type here]

over it again. So in fact what am I suggesting? Chapter one is the account of prehistoric Earth possibly with neanderthal and other prehistoric races being God's first creation. They needed no law because they were only able to speak or formulate concepts in relation to dominating their environment. Their main reason for being was the purpose of surviving and replenishing the Earth. But because their existence was devoid of any great capacity for the development of the soul; their intellectual capabilities were limited in scale to the proportion of consciousness they were able to develop. This is why we can find tools and rudimentary "art" but no great literature or writing. That is why brains are different and their bodies as well. They were given dominion over beasts and the reason necessary to carry out that function. But not able to grow in a way that could create an understanding which would manifest an awareness to their creator. They could know life through the act of

[Type here]

procreation and observing it but could not understand where it came from. They had enough intelligence to get food, make tools create groups and multiply but not enough of a soul to have an awareness of or relationship with God. Their prerogative was clear reproduce and survive. The formulation at the second man is much more detailed and there is an intimate connection immediately at his formation as the Lord God breathed into his nostrils. He must have been face to face. And that means there was a level of intimacy that our Lord God wanted from the beginning. Creating something and forming something are not the same thing. We use the words interchangeably, but its only for a matter of semantics. To create something means it was thought up and made out of a thought. To form something means we work with what is available to manufacture something. Chapter 2 :6 describing the formation process described in detail which lines up with delineating the elements (which already

[Type here]

existed from the first chapter of Genesis) of which man is composed of namely water and earth. The first chapter of Genesis just says they were in the image "them" as defined as the Us concept) But their elements were not mentioned nor was how the creation which they were brought into existence by. This implies either it's not important or it requires more reflection and scripture study for people to understand and receive a revelation about it. I will avoid trying to prove the idea of exactly what they were but even history admits there were different kinds of per-history species of mankind. And science and history just tell his that modern human just popped up and they all just "died out". This seems like a convenient but lazy explanation of what exactly happens. So, either science is not exact, or we are being deceived.

Let's look at Genesis 1: 28 where God says replenish the earth. We all know the prefix re means doing something again. So, if we continue to follow the specific

[Type here]

and detailed precision with which the scriptures are written we should pay careful attention to every word and detail equally with focus and awareness. Is Genesis 1:29 revealing to us a question to be posed? Are we to assume or believe that there were previous beings existing on another Earth in a previous iteration? That one word "replenish" changes the entire understanding of the possibility of creation accounts.

   As I said in the introduction of this book there will be more questions raised than answers given. I offer the readers and opportunity to explore these first two verses and expand their awareness as to the implications contained within the text on their own.

   Continuing with Genesis we see the battle lines being drawn between the seed of the Serpent and the seed of man Genesis 3: 15. God put enmity between the serpent seed and the seed of man. Where does the serpent seed come from? Are we to assume this means his cohort of

[Type here]

angels which fell from heaven in revelation? Revelation 12:4 "And his tail drew the third part of the stars of heaven and did cast them to the earth". And if God is Spirit and man is spirit and souls what does this mean the angels are? As we are made a little lower than the angels Hebrews 2:7 "Thou madest him a little lower than the angels". In what way were we made a little lower than the angels? A closer examination of Hebrews 2:9 reveals the answer "But we see Jesus, who was made a little lower than the angels for the suffering of death". So, we see that Our Lord Jesus was made a little lower than the angels so he would experience death, but in the process of death he was subjected to every suffering we experience before he actually died. In other words, to be made a little lower than the angels is to be **made for the purpose of suffering**, to understand what that means and through that suffering increase or soul's capacity to grow. I don't think that will sit well with most people of mainstream churchianity. But that is directly form scripture. And that is the only justification for suffering anyone can offer and still

[Type here]

explain the existence of God and suffering together. But as I have shown we are here to be deceived and that by extension implies suffering. We are not here to just enjoy life. We are to experience a vast range of ups and downs, gain and loss, joy and sadness so we can come to know God.

In Genesis chapter 4 verse 14 we see that Cain was driven out and he says that everyone who finds him shall slay or attempt to slay him. "Behold, thou hast driven me out this day from the face of the earth; and from thy face shall I be hid; and I shall be a fugitive and a vagabond in the earth; and it shall come to pass, that every one that findeth me shall slay me". Careful consideration shows there was in fact other people on the earth. Looking back in Genesis 1:26 and putting these verses together resolves the conflict of two different expressions of creation and gives insight into a way to solve how there could be other beings around that Cain would be worried about. If only Adam and Eve and his brother were those other people, he was worried about he could easily just leave and disappear.

[Type here]

There are Scholars and theologians who have invested many years in studying outside sources to explain away or justify their positions regarding the two different creation accounts, but I have never heard or seen one that completely resolves these questions. Gotquestion.Com proposes what's called the backtrack Theory, which we have observed. it is absurd considering the precision and detail of the other books and scripture.

Sitemap.Bibleodyssey.Com proposes there were actually two different authors. If this is true, then the entire Bible as the living and eternal Word of God becomes worthless and a book of lies. And there are too many consistencies and correlations for that to be true. According to biblical hermeneutics Stark exchange. Com says, "there is almost "Universal consensus" of critical Scholars at the two creation accounts coming from two different sources". Saying universal when it only applies to planet earth. And they know by saying Earthly consensus it would not sound

[Type here]

so authoritative and in fact would draw attention to the implication of the spiritual realm by mentioning it. Almost doesn't imply "is" as fact. It only is implying uncertainty. In addition, there was a time when scholars believed the Earth was flat according to "Universal consensus". There was a time when Scholars believed according to Universal consensus that the Earth was at the center of the solar system. And there have been many other times that scholars have "according to Universal consensus" have made claims about and then later had to change or they themselves had to backtrack on.

  One of the biggest deceptions manifested is the deception of our authority masquerading as truth. Acknowledgment of inconsistent authorship from the first two Chapters based on this precedent creates an acceptable precedent for continual compromise by institutions to systematically dismantle other parts of scripture. To suggest that someone wrote the first page

[Type here]

and then authorship with suddenly transferred to another person at random who wrote the other 99% of Genesis in addition to the other four books of the Pentateuch is just not believable. And knowing and therefore understanding the role of deception by our enemy which plays a role in the authority of the worldly systems I suggest that we consider both sides of these arguments with equal analytical fervor.

There is no analysis by Scholars given to the possibility of any other situation or circumstance even though the word "replenish" is clearly used at the first creation account. And not one scholar I have ever read addresses the reality in which Cain lived when he made his assertion about worrying regarding others who would find and kill him. Any possibility or reality of a possibility existing outside of mainstream scholarship would be to go against one's colleagues and the professional establishment and possibly tarnish one's reputation and

[Type here]

end their career as a scholar. For all their scholarship every scholar in their thesis about the two different creation accounts either miss the word "replenish" or chooses to ignore it as some random word chosen to use.

Deception is widespread throughout the higher educational institutions and people have a motive for agreeing with the mainstream status quo. After all, a PhD holder who is a so-called scholar doesn't want to go against the established ideologies of the world system and look like someone who can't conform. This is another example of willing ignorance out of a desire to avoid possibly being wrong. One of the sources for the reason of having two creation accounts is known as the Priestly source (also known as the y a h w i s t. Source) The name for that is a strange term considering the ancient Hebrews did not use vowels in their language and at the time of writing Genesis. In fact, according to Wikipedia: "There is almost no agreement on Yahweh's origins". So, the very name

[Type here]

for that version of explanation doesn't even make sense. Consensus among Universal Scholars is at best a coin toss. It is inconsistent and what is true today might be false tomorrow or what is false today might be true tomorrow. Science is in fact not exact. In fact, the word science comes from the Latin word scire which simply means to know. And even according to that origin word a lot of "science can't live up to. So, when someone says according to science all they're saying is according to what is known or more accurately according to the consensus of what is known. I lay no claim to possessing any more knowledge than a PhD holder or master's degree holder or someone who is a philosopher or professor at a college or high school. But as we know the problem with experts is they don't know what they don't know, and they seldom admit when they are wrong because they don't want to look as if they don't know something. Being able to conjugate a Hebrew verb to extract some deeper or

[Type here]

clearer understanding of what the word means or how it should be used or was used doesn't mean someone is entirely right when it comes to scripture. If This Were true, then the scripture would just be a book written by man and easy to understand. And anyone with a Strong's Concordance can look up the etymology of a word in Hebrew or Greek for themselves. I am not saying this is definitely why we have two creation accounts, but I am suggesting a possible reason for why. Which doesn't come from any scholarly background and is not from years of Main Street in indoctrination, (obviously) and desire to conform or propose an idea that everyone will agree with. I prefer to avoid an in-depth analysis as to how I personally perceive the passage in this analysis of scripture. But the there are ways to analyze scripture based on English which can become different after seeing the Greek or Hebrew root. But as mentioned there are not many inaccuracies according to Strong's concordance.

[Type here]

There are those who suggest that because the Bible was assembled under King James to establish control over his people and society was just a tool to establish a desired outcome, a means to an end. And yet others say that because the Old Testament comes from different time periods it's not relevant and lacks consistency throughout. And then there is inconclusive evidence of authorship of the four gospels and the Epistles in the New Testament. As well as other books. To all this I say- SO? No matter which perspective you choose to view from the fact is it still exists now and it's been poured out from printing presses more than any other book in the world. I want to bring to the page and awareness that if Jesus is the word of God and because of the invention of the printing press (very near the time of the King James which became the most widely used bible) and because of the printing press the King James version became popularly used is one heck of a coincidence. The tool specifically designed for the

[Type here]

reproduction of words so that they could be distributed throughout the world was used to reproduce God's word. According to ian. Wikipedia. Com as of 1995 the Bible holds the Guinness World Record for being the best sold book of all time with an estimated five billion copies. In addition to the Bible in addition the Bible is the most widely translated book in history. According to jw. Org over 90% of the Human family have access to at least part of the Bible in their own language. For all the scholars out there, I would like to provide those two facts about the popularity and need for the word of God in the world as a definitive "consensus". That consensus is based not on science or according to someone trying to fit in or conform or prove a theory for credit among peers, but by the human Collective consciousness humans.

The Bible in its current form arose out of the persecution of Christians from the early Roman emperors and the dark sadistic reign of the synagogue of evil known

[Type here]

as a Catholic church, which constantly changes its position on issues to conform to worldly standards. This inconsistency and desire to conform to the image of the world shows that they are not of the spirit of Truth and therefore not of the soul of Our Lord Jesus. To believe in that kind of organization which was responsible for the torture and mutilation as well as the intellectual deception of the population for many years is truly astounding and embodies the spirit of willing ignorance. As we shall see in the next chapter; the Catholic church and the propagation of the soul of ignorance spread to every denomination of believers which aspired to follow a right doctrine since Its inception. But what is the need for doctrine and why do we have it? What good does it do if we war not against the flesh but principalities? Why would we need a doctrine if we walk in the spirit? Isn't a Doctrine just a kind of ideology that must be conformed to in order to be qualified as a member of an

[Type here]

organization? Philippians 2:10-11 "that every tongue should confess that Jesus Christ is Lord, to the glory of God the Father" that should be enough doctrine. Jesus Himself clearly stated   do not add to or take away from his word. Deuteronomy 4:2

"You shall not add to the word that I command you, nor take from it, that you may keep the commandments of the LORD your God that I command you".

Deuteronomy

12:32 "Everything that I command you, you shall be careful to do. You shall not add to it or take from it" Any organization or church leader which creates a doctrine to follow is not following Jesus. In following doctrine, we are being led by the soul of deception and the soul of error. So ultimately doctrine in our faith comes from man being led astray by the deceiver.

[Type here]

[Type here]

Chapter 5

Where did the idea of Doctrine come from?

Where did the idea of a doctrine be required to have a right to have a relationship with God and his son come from?

This "doctrinism" has spread throughout all organized religion, from the beginning of the Catholic Church down to all the branches and denominations of modern-day churchianity.

[Type here]

Before we get into denominations and the differences, and their divisions let's look at how deception and the deceiver had his own strategy from the beginning.

   In the account of the beguiling of Eve why didn't the serpent address Adam? Why didn't Adam address the serpent? Maybe the serpent knew that by going through Eve he could get to Adam. Regardless of the reason the choice was made, one of the things that happened after the serpent deceived them was a division. A division was formed between not only Adam and Eve but between them and God as well. So, we see that one of the deceiver's tactics is causing division. His manipulation created an opportunity for God's design to activate. In the deceiver's mind he accomplished his goal, the destruction by Corruption of the Lord God's creation in total. In his mind he would now be able to become ruler of the world. As the two lines of seeds propagated there were races of humans which evolved different aptitudes and tendencies, we have we have list of people and what they were known for given in the first several chapters in Genesis as well as throughout Exodus as

[Type here]

well. As these races grew and possibly intermingled with the previous races that is those that Cain was speaking of in chapter four of Genesis. We see throughout the Old Testament the emergence of evil and corruption which leads to a point where God had enough and decided to wipe out most beings on the earth. Which shows that God was prone to such actions to reset the earth. All throughout the Old Testament There Is war and division as well as the worship of Idols like the golden calf (which never went away as evidence by its placing at Wall Street and other financial institutions of the world). All of Lucifer's cohorts created death, division and war for thousands of years. As Lucifer was enjoying his rain on Earth the prophecy of Jesus was fulfilled and Lucifer's solution to this problem was to kill him. Little did he know that it's exactly what God wanted. So, Lucifer even though he was an angel still lacked foresight. In fact, he acted exactly as he was supposed to. As the persecution of Jesus's followers continued, Lucifer continued to enjoy his temporary victory until he realized his mistake. By the time he realized what happened the soul of Jesus had already begun feeding the

[Type here]

Earth, so he created a way to use the faith of the believers of Jesus to his advantage. Without going into detail and getting into a history lesson I will summarize as quickly as possible in the next page the evolution of what is known as Christianity. It's important to note that until 300 A.D Christians were often killed and persecuted and generally regarded as an annoyance throughout the Roman Empire. Curiously though, around 300 A.D. the Roman emperor Constantine decided to legalize Christianity for whatever reason. After a couple of hundred years after the Catholic Church which supposedly started in 30 A.D took over the control as the prominent authority of the Christian religion in Europe and in the areas surrounding the countries of the Mediterranean In addition it established a Catholic Church in modern day turkey both of them sharing power in the world of religion. Around the 13th century a major shift occurred in hoe the Catholic church conducted policies regarding people who disagrees with the policies or doctrines and dogma of the church. Up to that time people were imprisoned or ostracized by the church for not conforming to their beliefs but after the beginning of the 13th

[Type here]

century the pope authorized imprisonment and other minor punishments to begin and as consequences to be implemented as a way to deal with anyone who believed other than what was taught according to their doctrine of faith. That was the beginning of the deceivers first form of influence. Up to this point, if anyone disagreed with the church they were seldom executed. But after the early part of the 13th century a major shift occurred within the Catholic church. It is ironic that the persecuted Christians became the creator of an organization that became the persecutors themselves. But this is part of how Lucifer gained a foothold into mainstream Christianity. During the period after the 4th Century to the 16th century the Catholic church dominated Europe. It became a force to collect taxes from people to implement rules and to control society. Not only did it control society, but it controlled kings and queens and almost all of the royal policy in Europe at that time. It is because of the Catholic church that we had wars known as Crusades against religions that were different from Christianity but as this is not a history lesson we won't talk about that in depth. One of the Kings in

[Type here]

the 16th names Henry 8th was not happy with his marriage and he wanted to marry another woman. But for him to get a divorce he had to get the approval from the Catholic Church. However, the Pope and none of his Cardinals would support King Henry the 8th and his request for a divorce. So, Henry the 8th decided that he would create his own church and break away from the Catholic church. This church was known as the Church of England which was also known as the Anglican Church. After the Anglican Church was formed there was a movement known as a Reformation which created two offshoots of the Anglican Church known as the Protestant church and in Germany called the Baptist Church in Holland. Both churches broke away out of a desire to worship as they saw fit without being told how to worship or what they should believe according to the doctrine or dogma of man or an earth-based seat of power. Ironically these two churches developed their own doctrine which then became binding to people who wanted to be a part of them, and they had to subscribe to the doctrine of belief which these churches established. So, from the beginning of organized religion the

[Type here]

very first Church established in the world according to the principles of the teachings of Jesus and his disciples was infiltrated by the soul of the deceiver. It's interesting that both Protestantism and Baptism emerged from the Anglican Church as a result of the desire to divorce-which is a form of division. This will be important, and we will come back to it. As the country across the Atlantic Ocean became more widely known by the by Europe and the Catholic Church the religion of the Catholicism became the forerunner of the spread of Christianity because of Spain and their arrival in the Americas and other parts of the world. And Spain was joined with the Catholic church and so received funding and resources from the Catholic church. Because of access to all these resources they had access to means to cross the ocean Atlantic Ocean and explore the North and South Americas and distribute their influence and religion. It became the prominent religious force in certain parts of the Americas, mainly he south of America. Later after the 1600s as more and more Europeans from England and Germany as well as Holland arrived in America and their religious beliefs and doctrines arrived with them.
[Type here]

This gave rise to endless denominations which continues to grow and divide and today the offshoots of these three religious organizations are in the hundreds and have membership and allegiance to worldly associations and affiliations attached to various enterprises in which they are still involved. A white paper from the Christian economics Forum estimates that churches in the United States have about 1 trillion dollars in real estate. Although churches are a non-profit organization, they can create subsidiaries which are separate legal entities from the church which can carry out taxable activities and generate income which means profits. The churches can then receive profits such as dividends. In other words, churchianity is big business in America. Let's look at some of the ministries and their church leaders to see how big the business of churchianity really is.

The Atlanta-based Ministry known as World Changers Church International's leader is the director Creflo Dollar. He makes between $50, 000 to $100, 000 per speaking event. He
[Type here]

is the sixth richest Pastor in the in the world. With a net worth of 30 million dollars (www.wealthypersons.com). Mr. Dollar actually asked his ministry congregation of about 200, 000 members to each contribute only $300 so that he could buy a 65 million dollars G650 jet. In addition to his jet, he has a Rolls-Royce and a few mansions.

Joel Olsteen: If anyone has ever seen this man, they should instantly be able to perceive something is just not quite right with him. He has squinty eyes and for some reason constantly blinks. An internet search gives varying amounts, and nobody is certain of his wealth. His net worth is listed from anywhere to 40 million to 100 million dollars, so the fact that his net worth is clouded in an uncertainty raises questions.

Chris Oyakhilome, a businessman with not only real estate holdings but also TV stations and his net worth is 50 million dollars.

[Type here]

Bishop TD Jakes a Bishop out of Texas he is worth 20 million dollars. According to Forbes magazine he has entered into a 1 billion dollar deal with Wells Fargo.(https://www.forbes.com/sites/jabariyoung/2024/02/13/inside-td-jakes-1-billion-partnership-with-wells-fargo/)

   Kenneth Copeland, according to the New York Post his net worth could up to 760 million dollars. I invite the reader to do their own research and see for themselves how lucrative the churchianity business in America really can be. These are just a few of the elite. There are other church leaders whose average income easily exceeds a million dollars.

[Type here]

As wealthy as these men are, they continue to accumulate more and more wealth. Arguments can be made that they do in fact help communities but to what degree and how proportionate that help is given compared to the standard of their wealth is in question. Some of these men own planes and mansions, so it's not as if they are living humbly or moderately living. They are living lavish lifestyles and are mingling with the elites of the world system.

Perhaps in the future I will write another book with much more information and details with many so-called church leaders and their wealth. I would like to clarify the purpose of mentioning all this. I only want to draw attention to the fact that as Jesus says we should lay out for ourselves Treasures in Heaven. These men clearly are not laying up treasures in heaven but rather treasures on Earth. It is true these men do actually provide some guidance and to some people, but for someone to attend these churches knowing the obscene wealth their shepherds possess and the things they ask of their congregation it would be an act of willing ignorance to

[Type here]

attend and participate in what they are doing. It is essentially spiritual snake oil.

For many years after the death of Christ, his apostles gave and received several scrolls, sharing them among different groups. Some were passed independently from one another until eventually various "church councils" began to come together around 320 A.D. to determine which books were authentic and had divine inspiration behind them. basically, to decide what to believe. That was the first attempt to establish a doctrine of belief.

In 325 AD, the first council of Nicaea was convened by Emperor Constantine in modern-day Turkey. This is where the first loose collection of writings was collated as a forerunner which served as a foundation for later Bibles. Most of the scriptures used were of the New Testament. Around 400 AD the New Testament was officially recognized and used in mass as church scripture. The New Testament was just loosely compiled mound of papers organized in a binder. The Old Testament was still being used among Hebrews (Jewish

[Type here]

people). But of course, they were used separately. Among Hebrews not the Catholic church at that time. But the Hebrew scrolls did in fact began being translated into Greek around 300 BC. Around the 5th century AD Saint Jerome translated not only the New testaments but Old testaments as well into one book known as the Vulgate, A Bible in Latin designed specifically for the mass literally and figuratively. Fast forward to the early 1600s and King James of England decides to create an "authorized version" of the Bible. It is important to note that in the 1200 years between Jerome creating the Latin Bible and King James putting together the authorized version of the Bible there were many translations of different parts of the   Vulgate into different languages. I have omitted a lot of different aspects of the linguistic history in relation to the translation of the Bible on its Journey from Saint Jerome's bible to becoming the King James's authorized version. The King James version established itself truly as the authorized version because for many years it has been the only   Bible version that has survived all of the changes within the churches over the last 400 years. Even though the three main
[Type here]

church denominations arose from different countries and spoke different languages the King James version was used among them since its inception. Despite all the manifestations of religious organizations the KJV remained the only Bible which organized religions used in mainstream churches in America until the 1960s. There have been approximately 20 other kinds of bibles since the publication of the KJV which disappeared into history because they were either written by individuals who weren't associated with any large body of believers or found to be lacking in accuracy or were part of denominations which didn't evolve. In America there has been an explosion of Bible versions over the 60 years and there are approximately 40 different versions in English in existence.

Today we have many different versions of the Bible all with slight variations which is another example of how the deceiver tries to create division among believers in Christ. In every iteration of God's word and the church on Earth there is a short period of unification and then the soul of the deceiver and the soul of division enters the church and spreads like a

[Type here]

virus creating more deception and more misconception. The various versions of English Bibles are not only an attempt to cash in on religion, but it attempts to create different views and confusion as to the true meaning of God's word. For the deceiver knows that people are easily distracted and manipulated and by creating a dizzying array of choices he creates options which manifest a sense of disorientation and petty bickering among different people regarding what could be considered right and wrong. Romans' chapters 12 and 14 deal with the differences in ideals among early apostolic believers of Christ. Everything that could be said about division arising from varying doctrines is said by Paul, so I encourage the reader to research that epistle. The heart of his message is plain "Be devoted to one another in love. Honor one another above yourselves." Romans 12:10. In other words live according to Jesus's example by sacrificing for one another. "Greater love has no one than this, than to lay down one's life for his friends", John 15:13

I don't see much of this in the modern age of the members

[Type here]

of the body of Christ. So why do people who know how much wealth these ministers are accumulating and how they accumulate that wealth attend the churches of these wealthy elitist Church ministers? The knowledge that these leaders use the money which is given to them to continue to lay up treasures not in the stores of Heaven but in the banks here on earth should repulse most believers and yet many people willingly ignore the deception. But why? It is possible this refusal to acknowledge the deception comes from not being able to let go of long held beliefs and open their eyes and accept responsibility and being afraid of the temporary shame of error. These sheep are literally afraid to take a leap of faith into the unknown territory and demonstrate their love and trust in truth. It's easier to be led as a lamb to spiritual slaughter then to stand up and be a lion of light. Of course, another reason they ignore the truth is envy. The congregation of members want what their leaders have. It is out of jealousy and hope to attain the same thing that these members continue in their ignorance. And today money gives one credit, not only financially but in regard to how they are perceived.
[Type here]

The stature of wealth has somehow been congratulated with the intrinsic value of a person to society. The desire to possess what church leaders have, not according to those leaders' spiritual gifts but their worldly wealth creates a desire of among the congregation members to follow them. In a sense they are worshiping these men who are in fact false prophets Matthew 24: 4-14. "And Jesus answered and said to them: "Take heed that no one deceives you. *For many will come in My name".* Many churches of this age are literally slaughterhouses of the soul. There is no reason for the doctrines to be disputed because all these divisions are man-made; driven by a spirit of contention and strife which are in no way related to what Christ taught. The churches today are offshoots of that which has been controlling men's souls for hundreds of years leading them to destruction and not salvation. The only doctrine is the word that Our Lord Jesus spoke. He explained that the faith and love he brings transcends all doctrine-Mathew 22;36-40" Master, which is the great commandment in the law? Jesus said unto him,

[Type here]

thou shalt love the Lord thy God with all thy heart, and with all thy soul, and with all thy mind". What is so difficult to understand about that? Everything he did was to fulfill the prophecies and become a conduit for the release of God's grace to be poured out into the world. To expect our Salvation to be premised on conforming to any other doctrine given to us by Jesus himself is Antichrist, as it is truly against what he taught and in contradiction to the word of God. While it's true that he did say John 3: 5 "Verily, verily, I say unto thee, except a man be born of water and of the Spirit, he cannot enter into the kingdom of God". It is self-evident according to Mathew 22;36-40 that even baptism is transcended by a person's love of God and devotion to him. Nowhere in the Bible does Jesus say unless you get baptized you can't get salvation. He just says unless a man be born of water and spirit. That does not imply the ritual of baptism. In John 3: 6 "That which is born of the flesh is flesh; and that which is born of the Spirit is spirit Marvel not that I said unto thee, Ye must be born again. Nicodemus answered and said unto him, how

[Type here]

can these things be? Jesus answered and said unto him, Art thou a master of Israel, and knowest not these things?" Nicodemus was a very intelligent man, and the way Jesus addresses him and asks him "are you not a master of Israel and yet don't understand"? Shows he was above an average understanding of the law and rituals. It seems that Nicodemus would be aware of the role of cleansing rituals since those were common in Israel, so being "born of water" must have some unknown meaning that we must receive revelation about to fully comprehend. The use of water is a common practice of "cleansing" and purifying sacrifices to make clean in preparation for presenting them to God. Maybe what is meant by being "born of water" is not literal baptism by water but being baptized in cleansing power of the blood of his sacrifice through faith in his sacrifice. In1 Peter 1:22 we read "Since you have in obedience to the truth purified your souls for a sincere love of the brethren, fervently love one another from the heart". In this passage Peter uses obedience to truth as that which purifies and cleanses-that is baptizes the believers.

[Type here]

Hebrews 9:14

"How much more will the *blood of Christ,* who through the eternal Spirit offered Himself without blemish to God, to *cleanse your conscience* from dead works to serve the living God"?.

This is just an observation after all, Jesus himself was baptized by John. But perhaps Jesus was the only one who needed to be baptized and cleansed ritually since he was to be offered directly to God as a last "propitiation" to be offered from the world. 1John 2:2 "And he is the *propitiation* for our sins: and not for ours only, but also for the sins of the whole world". The word propitiation means to escape the wrath of God. It was done to appease anger to reconcile the relationship with God. It is done by offering sacrifices to God. For those who often use the example of an angry jealous wrathful God in the Old Testament as a contradiction to the God of the New Testament as proof that there is an inconsistency in the word, I suggest increasing your knowledge of the word to understand it more clearly. It is the fear of God which is truly the beginning of wisdom.
[Type here]

We constantly use the understanding of Earthly ideals to understand spiritual ideals and think they supersede God's will and word. What can the act of being dunked underwater compared to the baptism in the blood of the Lambs sacrifice? Such details are minute. It's like trying to kill a mosquito with a frying pan- just stop. We live in a time when half a dozen church leaders have enough wealth to help every member of their congregation and still have enough to be happy. These church leaders today could lay up much wealth in the storehouse of our heavenly father, but they choose instead to pursue a life of being worshiped but at the same time they are shackled by the fettered from the greed which results in economic bondage. They are living examples of wolves in sheep's clothing and yet their own members can't see enough to perceive. It is the epitome of the abomination of desolation. The desolation of our time is the wasteland of souls in the churches and the abomination is the in-habitation of Lucifer within the walls of our churches.

The core of Jesus is teaching is giving and through that giving experience the joy of sacrifice out of love. And in all his
[Type here]

examples and parables the one aspect of most if not all have in common is the principle of increasing through sacrifice. Matthew 25:31- 36. 1 Kings 17, 2 Cor9:7, 1 Chronicles 29, Luke 6: 30, Matthew 10: 8, Luke 14:13-14, Matthew 19: 21-30. Mark 10:22-30. The number of scriptures about giving mentioned in the New Testament from the mouth of Jesus is at a much higher relation to almost all other ideals. God gave his son, and the son gave his life. We are to live according to that principle and by his example. Both gave out of love and took joy in it. As a personal testimony I feel fulfilled most when I give whether it be my time or money. But it is a giving done out of love and willingness in sharing because it not out of necessity or an obligation. It is for this reason that a distinction must be made between giving and sharing the same way there should be a distinction between obeying and willingly following. For example, when I pay a bill, I am giving money and I, like most people, do not take pleasure or have a cheerful soul when I am paying a bill. I do however derive a sense of accomplishment from satisfying a sense of my responsibility as a member to my community. Sharing on the

[Type here]

other hand is done out of a desire to spread your love and make others feel and appreciate what you have so they can directly experience joy. The distinction between giving out of willingness or sharing extends from the financial to the heavenly realms in terms of serving the God.

 In truth, if an abundance of any material gifts or blessings is what one expects to get from giving then that individual is off course. If when someone prays it is "help me give me, I want" then they can expect to receive something but they will receive nothing. Because the blessings we receive come from come from Treasures in Heaven. The store of value in heaven is full of non-material assets which is the currency of the kingdom of God. Our actions in this world are reflections of our spiritual store of values. From our personal treasury withdrawals are made to exchange not material things but more heavenly Investments, of which the return on accrues interest and is compounded daily according to our thoughts and deeds.

[Type here]

In our current age of commerce, it seems Bitcoin is all the rage. Bitcoin has a rate of return higher than any other asset, mainly because of an unexplained rocket in price over the last year. In terms of spiritual value; sharing would be the equivalent of investing in a kind of spiritual BTC. For those who are morally bankrupt it is because their storehouse of value is empty and will remain so until they come to the Knowledge of God. In the material world the manifestation of Our Lord's investment in humanity through his sacrifice yielded a heavenly return as stewardship of this world and our souls. In scripture we read of Jesus's temptation in the Wilderness in Matthew Chapter 4:1-11. He e refuses all three of the material temptations of our material world. At The Last temptation he was offered power over all the kingdoms of the world. Lucifer couldn't see the plan of God at work because if he had he would have foreseen that Jesus was already in place to receive all the kingdoms of the world. And if Lucifer knew this, he would not have engineered Jesus's death to destroy the world. All these accounts of how Jesus was offered material assets of

[Type here]

the world and yet refused all of them shows he acted not out of a need to obey, but out of a willingness to follow.

I look towards church leaders to emulate his actions of giving and sharing and sacrifice through their own sacrifice. But as we see there are some church leaders who lay up stores of treasure in Earth and not in heaven. As we have seen non-profit entities can funnel money into their coffers by establishing for-profit entities connected to their nonprofit organizations. The physical church is not the Church of Christ. He wasn't establishing a material establishment of a physical institution and structured buildings organized and designed to increase power and profit through the manipulation of man's soul. They are not our body of Christ.

The joy of giving cannot be taught or learned. Like most other gifts from God in particular the soul of Jesus- it must be accepted.

I read an analogy about accepting Jesus's sacrifice being likened to the difference of an employer asking if you want

[Type here]

your paycheck direct deposited and just automatically doing it. This analogy speaks for itself, but I will explain rather briefly for those who still don't understand. The difference between getting money via direct deposit and getting a check is that the money is already there in your account, all you need to do is spend it when you want to. You have access to it whenever you want and it was given to you without you having to decide or choose, in other words no effort. However, if paid with a check there is an effort required on your part to turn that check into currency by going to the bank or going to a check cashing service and then having access to the cash which you can spend. This is a very simple analogy but its effective. Another analogy is simply winning the lottery. You literally do nothing to receive a substantial amount of money. Of course, spending a dollar or any other monetary amount does require effort, but I think the point is made because what you receive in proportion to the effort you put in eclipses the energy spent by magnitudes. The effort is minimal and done with no thought and little regard to your actions taken. For human beings the odds of winning the lottery are astronomical but by

[Type here]

the grace of God and Our lord Jesus we are all winners of the Heavenly Lottery.

Chapter 6

Why do bad things happen?

As a faith-based person I get asked this question a lot. My answer is "I simply don't know". How can anyone really know why something bad happens to good people and children? I don't presume to know the mind of God. But I do know the mind of the deceiver. In fact, the more knowledge of God we have, we can gain more awareness of the deceiver and how he operates. Blaming the evil of the world which happens on the devil is to shift the blame and accountability of the choices people make onto someone else. It is difficult to pinpoint the reasons why people perpetuate darkness. But there are

[Type here]

people who do things which arise from an obvious possession of a destructive and malicious nature or corruption of the soul.

The origin of destructive force in a person is often attributed to some kind "consensus" among the scientific community which says it can arise from a chemistry imbalance of the brain or hormones, or some kind of traumatic event that a person experienced. There is no doubt these explanations more than suffice for a lot of plausible reasons of erratic and unstable behavior. There really can be no concrete explanation of a behavior that occurs from a corruption of the soul. There can't be in fact because desires and wants rise from an inconceivable and non-material place. And as we know we war against principalities Ephesians 6:10-8 "For we wrestle not against flesh and blood, but against principalities, against powers, against the rulers of the darkness of this world, against spiritual wickedness in high places". The prince of the air Ephesians chapter 2:2-4 "Wherein in time past ye walked according to the course of this world, according to the prince of the power of the air, the spirit that now worketh in

[Type here]

the children of disobedience" Lucifer is a prince of the air but Jesus is the Lord of the world and the souls therein. If it is true, that we are at war against unseen powers then clearly these powers are influences which manipulate and control us if we allow. We infer to these unseen principles as unclean spirits however this is not an accurate description as spirit is defined in Genesis Chapter 2:6 as that which God breathed into man. Therefore, there can be no unclean spirits. So, what are greed less gluttony and so-called sins? Sin is a Greek archery term which means to miss the mark so to speak in terms of sin is really to say that we have not achieved a goal that is in regard to growth of our soul achieving a goal set for us.

But who set the goal and where did the idea of the goal come from? I propose at conception the seed of consciousness is planted for a human to become not just a soul, but a living soul according to Genesis 2:7 "Then the Lord God formed a man[a] from the dust of the ground and breathed into his nostrils the breath of life, and the man became a living soul". The New international version uses the word "being" instead

[Type here]

of soul. Changing that one word takes away from the meaning contained in the text. It is in the marriage of the flesh, spirit and soul that man becomes a "living soul". For something to be alive it must be in existence and to be in existence in this world a material body is needed, and for that body to have life it must have a spirit. But a body with just a spirit would just be a "vegetable". So, for the finishing touch of our existence to be fully formed we need a soul to inhabit it. For it is this consciousness of soul which can organize and direct the process of cellular division.

As oxygen is required for all cellular activity this means the spirit of God is active at the moment of conception and conception is the moment when the soul begins to form. It is the soul that gives the capacity to experience a wide range of emotional states that life offers us through our daily interactions so that we can grow and understand what that capacity for growth as a soul means and relate to our Father in heaven and to Jesus Our Lord and brother. For God is a being that has the capacity to experience every range of emotion

[Type here]

and is capable of feeling all these emotions on a scale we cannot even begin to imagine. This is a possibility as to why there are so many different emotions expressed by God according to different situations in the Old Testament. God was able to be upset, angry, loving and forgiving as well as exhibit so many other human traits. As we are formed in the image of the   Lord God, we also have the capability to experience these ranges of motion because we were formed in his likeness. So, he can be jealous, he can be wrathful, and he can be envious, but he also has the capacity for love, forgiveness and empathy. So many people point out the contrast of God of the Old Testament with the God of the New Testament. But God in the New Testament is only mentioned by Jesus and God in the New Testament does nothing and is only mentioned in connection with Jesus. In fact, the god of the Old Testament seldom performs or does anything in the New Testament. Because everything that happened in the Old Testament was a foreshadow of what was to come in the form of our Lord Christ Jesus. To assume that a being capable of creating heaven and earth incapable of experiencing emotions

[Type here]

is to forget that we are formed in his image and have his spirit in us. In fact it is the opposite, a being that powerful would be able to experience every range of human emotion imaginable on a scale we can't imagine.

At this point from all the reading of the material in this book it should be self-evident that we often see with our eyes but don't perceive, and hear with our ears but don't understand. Truly this is a reality we live in and experience because of the distractions and deceptions of the world system. We use words about evil and good in casual conversation, but we have forgotten how real the meaning behind them is. The radio commentary personality Paul Harvey made an astounding prediction in the form of a warning on his commentary show "The Rest of the story". It was in one of his broadcasts entitled was how "If I were the Devil". What follows on the following page is a transcript of his broadcast.

[Type here]

"If I were the devil … If I were the Prince of Darkness, I'd want to engulf the whole world in darkness. And I'd have a third of its real estate, and four-fifths of its population, but I wouldn't be happy until I had seized the ripest apple on the tree — Thee. So, I'd set about however necessary to take over the United States. I'd subvert the churches first — I'd begin with a campaign of whispers. With the wisdom of a serpent, I would whisper to you as I whispered to Eve: 'Do as you please.'

"To the young, I would whisper that 'The Bible is a myth.' I would convince them that man created God instead of the other way around. I would confide that what's bad is good, and what's good is 'square.' And the old, I would teach to pray, after me, 'Our Father, which art in Washington…'
"And then I'd get organized. I'd educate authors in how to make lurid literature exciting, so that anything else would appear dull and uninteresting. I'd threaten TV with dirtier movies and vice versa. I'd pedal narcotics to whom I could. I'd sell alcohol to ladies and gentlemen of distinction. I'd tranquilize the rest with pills.

[Type here]

"If I were the devil, I'd soon have families that war with themselves, churches at war with themselves, and nations at war with themselves; until each in its turn was consumed. And with promises of higher ratings, I'd have mesmerizing media fanning the flames. If I were the devil, I would encourage schools to refine young intellects, but neglect to discipline emotions — just let those run wild, until before you knew it, you'd have to have drug sniffing dogs and metal detectors at every schoolhouse door.

"Within a decade I'd have prisons overflowing, I'd have judges promoting pornography — soon I could evict God from the courthouse, then from the schoolhouse, and then from the houses of Congress. And in His own churches I would substitute psychology for religion and deify science. I would lure priests and pastors into misusing boys and girls, and church money. If I were the devil, I'd make the symbols of Easter an egg and the symbol of Christmas a bottle.

"If I were the devil, I'd take from those who have, and give to those who want until I had killed the incentive of the ambitious.

[Type here]

And what do you bet I could get whole states to promote gambling as the way to get rich? I would caution against extremes and hard work in Patriotism, in moral conduct. I would convince the young that marriage is old-fashioned, that swinging is more fun, that what you see on the TV is the way to be. And thus, I could undress you in public, and I could lure you into bed with diseases for which there is no cure. In other words, if I were the devil, I'd just keep right on doing what he's doing.

Paul Harvey, good day."

This was broadcast in 1965 and how prophetic it was. How accurate and pertinent this warning was. Our adversary is real, it's not just a metaphor. It's not something made up to control Society in fact the idea that it was made up to control Society was created by it to manipulate society.

This manipulation of society though religion began with the Catholic Church through their control of knowledge and the spread of ignorance throughout the world at that time. At one point they were selling the forgiveness of sins, this practice

[Type here]

was known as "Indulgences" and it was literally people giving money to the church to receive forgiveness for sins. I won't attempt to expound on that because it shows the deception that was promoted by the Catholic church without needing any extra effort.   Considering the effects, the Catholic church on society it is a miracle we managed to crawl out of that age and into the age of enlightenment. For it is from the enlightenment that the Industrial Age and the rapid rise of technology manifested itself more and more. There are those who would argue that the Age of Enlightenment produce works of art and music that are some of the most beautiful expressions of the human soul in the world. And as Beauty comes from truth it cannot be corrupt or bad. However, we have seen already know how sight and sound can be manipulated into projecting a form of beauty but not coming from truth. For beauty is an expression based on the appearance of a thing, it is not defined by its ethics, and it is not defined by its sense of manifestation of truth in the world. It is only defined by the effort it took to create it and how pleasing it is to the eye. All the discussions about proportions

[Type here]

and scales are still just regarding appearances. Art could be considered the domain of Lucifer as he was counted among the most beautiful angels in heaven. So make of that in relation to art as you will. But the Art industry is just as deceptive as any other industry. Why do some art pieces sell for hundreds of thousands of dollars and sone sell for ten dollars? It is an industry that is totally subjective so the in this light the conversation of truth in relation to beauty is irrelevant.

There have been many discourses of philosophers during the age of enlightenment from commentaries on classical Greek culture. They talk about art and beauty being expressions of truth, but these expressions of truth are formed from the idea of men about how something should look and therefore or not really expressions of truth. And we should always be reminded that appearances can be deceiving. We should also remember that the cleverest of lies can be presented as truth. From the Age of Enlightenment rose new expressions of freedom and new ways to perceive reality which opened the world up to

[Type here]

even more forms of deception. God's influence was at work during these times manifesting his own tools of warfare. One of the greatest tools which he has ever manifested is the tool of the printing press. For it was by God's will from working though men in the realm of the soul and acting on persons not only of power such as King James but great minds of the time such as the creator of the printing press that a tool manifested which could bring about the spread of God's word known as the Bible. For it is quite a coincidence that a tool designed specifically for increasing the printing capability and distribution of knowledge was created and the first book printed was a Bible. How coincidental is that?

A tool specifically designed for the reproduction of the written word was invented and the first book printed was a bible-the word of God. For as Jesus is the word and the Bible is the word of God the soul of Jesus is contained in the Bible and because of a tool that was created to spread the written word. God's will be able to spread throughout the world and yet the deceiver was able to manipulate and control the dissemination

[Type here]

of that information. To this day by, Lucifer is occupying the very houses which the soul of Jesus is supposed to be occupying not only physically but in essence. For as humans have the function of the body of Christ, we are The Living Church. We can be subjected to in habitation not only of our own souls but by the soul of Jesus as well as principalities of the air.

I hope by now you have begun to realize what the world is facing. I hope you read the words from a person who has no affiliation or no motivation to seem right or to promote an agenda or any connection to any religious organization other than the members of the body of Christ. As I've said previously my only intention is to build awareness as to other possible realities that are existing around us. My sincere hope is that you take time and truly reflect and, in that reflection, receive revelation about the world we are living in and about the life you live.

So why do bad things happen? I have my own question for people who ask this. Why do people need to know why bad things happen? And if something bad does happen why do
[Type here]

people need to blame anyone for something bad that happens? As we have seen the need for blame to shift responsibility and accountability originated from the very beginning. If acceptance is the pillar of our faith, then we are to accept the good and bad as it comes. People philosophize God's workings as if we could even begin to understand his will in its totality. That attempt to understand is an attempt to build a personal Tower of Babel of understanding. It is built on lack of humility and lack of the awareness of God. To argue from a moralistic standpoint is to come from a human position of understanding which will not yield any results which aren't circular. The idea of God being powerful and in everything but not allowing evil should stop at the idea of God's plan of redemption. Insert Romans chapter 8:28 "And we know that all things work together for good to them that love God, to them who are the called according to his purpose". There is no need to philosophize and analyze. The only thing people who are faith-based need to do is accept. Except the bible, accept the origins of death and corruption, accept what Jesus said and accept his Soul of holiness and continue in faith daily.

[Type here]

The idea of morals is man-made which are not absolutes but only relative concepts in the world. If they were absolute, then the law would not be blind to them. The law has no ethic other than what is provable, and the evidence presented. And as Paul wrote in Romans 7:4 "Wherefore, my brethren, ye also are become dead to the law by the body of Christ; that ye should be married to another, even to him who is raised from the dead, that we should bring forth fruit unto God". Any man-made law given becomes irrelevant to a being in the body of Christ not because of being better or superior but because doing something contrary to a man-made ethic would not occur to the mind of someone living according to the soul of holiness with an awareness to God's spirit being in them. Living according to the awareness that we are each accountable to a higher power means much more than being controlled by a law on Earth.

Remember, that the word holy means set apart for a specific purpose. So, what power to does the law have over someone who is not part of the world because they are set

[Type here]

apart from it. In fact, it seems like laws exist so people can break them not to protect people. I do not advocate anarchy or revolution, I only express that we as members of the Body of Christ freely follow that which is right according to the Holy soul released by Jesus's example of sacrifice.

I do not use the word holy spirit because God's spirit gives life to everything that respires and gives life to anything that helps life propagate. It was given at birth to everything born including the world. The gift of life doesn't come from the world, so it is already holy in and of itself. And cannot be made more holy by any act of man or nature. It is the soul that has the capacity for growth. Therefore, I propose a new paradigm in which instead of holy spirit we say holy soul, for we are born with a living soul, but it must be made holy through acceptance. The word spirit is often used to express the intangible unseen world from which influences arise and while I agree that there is a reality that is unseen and yet existing in which the habitation of God resides in which we call Heaven I do not agree that any being such as Lucifer has a spirit as they

[Type here]

exist from before the foundations of the world and are not in need of any organs of perception or of the respiration process. Therefore, they are not made of spirit but are made of a kind of consciousness which is what are soul comes from. For as man was made little lower than the angels by experiencing death as in Hebrews 2:6 "But one in a certain place testified, saying, what is man, that thou art mindful of him? or the son of man that thou visitest him?" Thou madest him a little lower than the angels; thou crownedst him with glory and honour, and didst set him over the works of thy hands." and finally we read "But we see Jesus, who was made a little lower than the angels for the suffering of death, crowned with glory and honour; that he by the grace of God should taste death for every man".

As we have discussed it is by death, we are made a little lower than the angels, and so Jesus came to Earth in our form so he too could be made subjected to death. So, if we are made a little lower than the angels by the experience of death then their status above us is because they can't experience

[Type here]

death. They must exist in some form. It is not spiritual because God is spirit moving in all life on earth. Is it possible they exist as souls created by God? As we are distinctly called "living" souls because we have a body and can die. And this is why we made a little lower than them. Perhaps they are not living souls because they can't grow in the same way we can and maybe this was the cause of the rebellion? I admit wholeheartedly at this point this is completely my own conjecture and so it is only a speculative theory. But it does say in revelations12:7-17 "And the great dragon was cast out, that old serpent, called the Devil, and Satan, which deceiveth the whole world: he was cast out into the earth, and his angels were cast out with him." So according to scripture they have been here the entire time man has been here. It explains how a person can be "possessed" to do something. Before we can down this road though remember, we often take for granted the idea of possession. But we use it in out vocabulary often. A perfect example would be the question, "What possessed you to do that"? For it is not from the spirit that thoughts arise but from consciousness which resides in the seat of the Soul. If this

[Type here]

is true than there are a very large number of beings that exists around us capable of influencing human behavior on a degree that would explain the facilitation of all the deception and manipulation of mankind. It also explains the evolution of a "guided" formation of the world system and the technology that has grown rapidly in the last two thousand years.

For as humans are made of a brain which is the center of the nervous system which facilitates light transfer, we are literally beings of light housed in material form. That which we call soul is in fact a body of light made of consciousness that is given life through the spirit of God which is breath. All things that breathe and respire no matter if it is a tree a fish an animal or a human have the spirit of God within them and without that Spirit have no life. For it is in this way that God's spirit is in all things.

Our Lord and Savior Christ Jesus is a manifestation of a soul formed by that spirit through that spirit which the materialization of in this reality gave man an opportunity to join, so that man could draw closer to God through the organs

[Type here]

of perception which are a gateway of the soul. And through his sacrifice offered man the opportunity to join closer to that spirit to have a new and higher experience of God's soul. Because in this form we can only experience it in a way obscured by material reality. For as Paul said in one Corinthians chapter 13 :12 "For now we see through a glass, darkly; but then face to face: now I know in part; but then shall I know even as also I am known". As our awareness of God's spirit increases his awareness of us increases and we are known by him even more. This creates a self-feeding loop in which our understanding of his nature grows because he helps us to better understand ourselves more deeply and where we come from. Which creates deeper understanding of his nature, this gives us access to the ability to view ourselves from a point which is outside of ourselves.

The objectivity which is created begins the process of operating from a point of truth viewing things such as a reporter who looks through a lens. Our evolution is such that we start from the reporter looking through a camera being

[Type here]

behind a lens of objectivity and slowly become the lens itself. And the sacrifice of Jesus offered the opportunity to share in a perpetuation of a higher frequency of being in which the soul instead of sleeping at physical death can resurrect into an experience of being which draws is existence not through a process of physical organs interfacing with God's spirit on Earth but directly touching it joining it with its essence. It is for this reason that we must first acknowledge God and more so the reality of his spirit so that we can then come to acknowledge his son and can experience a revitalization of our soul. So that it may increase daily so that it has the capacity to take part and the kingdom that is to come. Our actions committed daily and the way we feed our soul will determine the degree to which we are able to partake in the activities of the Kingdom to come.

Therefore, Believers in Christ have no need of man's law to distinguish from right and wrong and conform to a worldly system. Being part of the body of Christ and being conjoined with the Holy Soul implies that a person has accepted being

[Type here]

A.A. Antunes

set apart from worldly values and principles and strives to achieve a closer union with the spirit of God. If a person truly and wholeheartedly has been grafted into the soul of Jesus, they are not able to use worldly logic to rationalize or Justify God and have no need to. Therefore, the idea of why bad things happen has no relevance to them. The fact that something happens does imply there is a rational explanation for it happening because we live in a cause-and-effect related world. But ultimate nobody can explain exactly why they do why they do. The reasons of our choices stem from something unknown and yet the fact that it does exist in and of itself proves there are forces operating beyond our realm of physical perception. Attempting to explain these are always bound to degenerate into a Satan mind set whereas the word Satan means accuser. People always need someone or something to blame. Blaming God for bad things which happen is like blaming Henry Ford for every accident and death that occurs from automobiles. A prime mover or a first cause does not imply continuous interaction with the effect and often the prime mover of down chain causes and effects -

[Type here]

while related in occurrence have no connection to bearing the responsibility of the aftermath.

Do angels and God intervene in the affairs of men? Yes of course. But only when he chooses to and for his own reasons. Those in the body of Christ who truly walk by faith can experience a reality where God intervenes (or is more likely to intervene) on a higher frequency. Millions of people have testimonies of how God has worked in their lives. Whether they believe or not. There are so-called unexplained events which happen to random people who later realize they are part of God's family and come to know Christ. In fact, why would God help somebody who doesn't believe in his existence? If you were to ignore a friend or family member and didn't have a good mutual relationship, would you be apt to help them if they asked? In fact, would you think to ask that person for help? Our relationship with God and Jesus is no different. The world has created a rift between man and God and Jesus. For we three are the trinity of reality and existence. Because it is not the spirit, which is made holy, it is the soul.

[Type here]

We continue to separate ourselves and externalize our relationships with our Father in heaven and our brother Jesus.

The bad things that happen in the world, the atrocities, the loss of life of the innocent ones, the brutal realities that we have to face and the horrors that people inflict on each other creates pain and suffering. The pain a parent experiences when they lose a child cannot be expressed with any words. It can only be expressed with tears of grief and sorrow and the suffering that goes along with it will never truly disappear but from the pain and through the growth of the soul that comes with dealing with it people acquire a greater capacity to love. God does not allow suffering God creates suffering. We must accept all things if we accept God's grace. As God gives grace freely to all we must accept all things with grace. If we do not accept the so-called bad with the good then grace is not grace of God, which we should embody which as members of the body of Christ should possess.

To accept something with grace or to be graceful does not involve moving a certain way or looking a certain way. In fact,

[Type here]

that association of grace in life is a kind of seduction. Giving grace is an extension of the soul through compassion and love and unbounded empathy. We must first extend grace to ourselves before we can extend it to others. We must accept God as being everywhere and all around us, and next accept the reality of Jesus as being our Lord and Savior and finally accepting ourselves for where we come from who we really are and what we have the capacity to be. I know the concept of God wanting people to suffer sounds radical and completely against him loving us.

To say all things work to the glory of God when a four-year-old gets cancer and dies is difficult to see how this can be true. But what we don't see are the effects the next day or the next week or the next month because that happened. Because of the dynamics in the relationships of the people around that child going through that experience. Every horrendous act, every atrocious crime is committed through the lack of agency a person has over themselves. This implies and outside force working through them. I have repeatedly stated the darkness

[Type here]

is real and Lucifer is real and the battle for the soul of mankind and Earth is real. And ultimately this is why bad things happen. But it's because God wants it to happen. For we truly war not against the flesh but against principalities and powers of the air and things unseen. How do we fight this war? Proverbs 4:7 ". Wisdom is the principal thing; therefore, get wisdom: and with all thy getting get understanding" Embrace this and acknowledge it and it will change the perception of your reality and your relationship with God. It would be redundant to say that God allows suffering to test our faith. And in some way this statement is true, for without being put in a position where a person must struggle, they will never become stronger, and this applies to every interaction and thing that grows. I suggest that a lot of the suffering in the world is man-made and the result of willing ignorance. Willing ignorance in the world is promoted by the world system and its various outlets such as media, entertainment, religious organization, and educational institutions. And as we have seen these organizations are being empowered and enlivened by unseen forces which do not have any desire except to destroy us.

[Type here]

As God is the root of creation, we must accept that all goodness and evil, all joy and suffering originate with God, and all is created for the glory of God.

God's glory is often equated with light and brightness and true. Of which man-made art is a pale reflection of. Psalms 19:1 "The heavens declare the glory of God; and the firmament sheweth his handywork". In Psalms 113:4 "The Lord is high above all nations, and his glory above the heavens". And Isaiah chapter 60:1-5 "arise shine, for your light has come and the glory of the Lord Rises upon you". And John 1:14 "And the Word was made flesh, and dwelt among us, (and we beheld his glory, the glory as of the only begotten of the Father,) full of grace and truth". We see grace and truth associated with God's glory. It is for God's glory that man exists so that we may share in it and experience it directly instead of observing it from outside As Jesus suffered, so should we so that we could understand through empathy and learn to have compassion and forgive.

[Type here]

We worship grace, truth and light not because they are the opposite of darkness and deception but because it is how we as members of Christ honor God's Glory.

Peace be unto you and always remember. God is real and Our Lord Jesus is real. Remember

Chapter 7

Free will

[Type here]

This subject wasn't originally intended for this book but it was included at the end as an afterthought about what I as a person think. Most people say as a writer you should stay objective and only use facts, but I disagree. If people can't understand me as a person and only see the words I write they won't have a direct insight into how I as the author think. So much as been written on this topic by people smarter than I am and a lot of what they say confuses me. In scripture when Paul writes on faith it can take wuite a while to digest what he means and I don't think I am alone when I say sometimes...it just confuses me.

I want to state what I think with the hope that other members of The Body of Christ can have a different commentary on it and consider the matter in a more simplified way.

So, I will just begin by saying free will is one of those issues that has arisen from man trying to understand the soul of God by bringing his intellect to the matter instead of arriving at

[Type here]

clarity through reflection. By first asking God to give clarity on a subject you will have better results than just diving in and analyzing data like a machine. It has caused a lot of debate and division among the family of believers over the centuries. And it is something that is another distraction and trick up the deciever's sleeve in an effort to ensnare the willingly ignorant.

Most of the division within the body of Christ is a result of deception to manipulate the willingly ignorant and the gullible, that is, those willing to believe anything out of their thirst and hunger for the knowledge of God

The idea that free will cannot exist in a world that has an all-powerful creator and all-knowing creator, and all present creator is an untruth. To begin with nowhere in the scripture does God say anywhere ;"hear me, I am All knowing all powerful and All present" as if he is the wizard behind the curtain in the land of Oz. This viewpoint of God has been something which is assumed because when people read scripture that's what they get out of it. And then the propaganda machine and the devices of Lucifer get this

[Type here]

concept into the minds of people and a narrative is created which perpetuates until it is the norm of the belief system. I have used three different AI tools and asks specifically, where in the Bible does God say he is All knowing or All powerful or All Present? Every time it's the same answer. There is nowhere in scripture where God says that or anyone else. Even if you use different search engines the results are the same. In fact God portrays himself has a very human God. He has the feelings of jealousy, hate, anger, curiosity Jeremiah 17:10 " I the Lord search the heart, I try the reigns, even to give every man according to his ways, and according to the fruit of his doings."

So the idea of God being some Thanos type figure out of a Marvel film is in error. His capacity for human emotion is beyond our comprehension. To assume that he is any way is to miss his meaning in the "I am" statement to Moses on the exodus story.

I get a lot of questions about God and free will and suffering and they usually start off with "If God ..then why?" My first

[Type here]

response is what makes you think I am an authority on God? My next question is why you are asking me and not him"

 In scripture Acts 17:28 it says "For in him we live and move and have our being in him". Does that mean God is everywhere? No, it means exactly what it says it means. We live in him and have life because of him and exist because of him. That doesn't mean he is omnipresent as *we think it means.* That is just an assumption we make from using our brains instead of our minds. People try so hard to get meaning out of something but all it takes it just asking God directly what somethings means and being open to how he reveals himself in what you see around you. If he created the heavens and the Earth doesn't that make him all powerful? Why should that make him all powerful? It means he has tremendous creative influence in everything but that make him all powerful. Mathew 19-26 "With God all things are possible". So does that statement make "All Powerful''. No it doesn't mean God is All powerful, it means that whatever is possible it is possible because of God. And then there is the question of

[Type here]

suffering, but as already addresses in previous chapters, suffering was created by man FORGETTING what God told him and using his agency in a way that was contrary to what he was told. And if God knows everything before it happens then why would he even bother to create all this? Anyone who asks that question must be very unhappy with their life and who they are. My simple is answer: because he can. All my answers come from a place of accepting God's word and believing not because of empirical data,(although from my experience the data I do have is more than enough proof) but moreso from faith. If a person truly has fear of God it is because they are aware of his existence, that awareness will lead to knowledge and then understanding and finally wisdom. But not wisdom like an old Chinese monk in a kung fu movie. Wisdom as in understanding what it means to have a relationship with Our father and his Son- The LIVING WORD.

Returning to the subject of free will. So if God is all powerful than how can free will exist if already knows what will happen before it does. Well as I have already shown nowhere does it

[Type here]

say in scripture that God is all powerful. But if he really was all powerful the answer is simple. **An all powerful being can create any reality it wants to**. The answer is in the question.

But I will play along with this question for the sake of a mental exercise. If God is all knowing and he predtermined everything we would still have agency. Even if every choice you ever made was predestined you still have the *freedom* to make that choice in your life because of more than one option to choose from. God is not making those choices, *you ar.e* If there was a Coke and a 7UP in front of you and you were predestined to drink the coke *you* made the choice and there is always the option because there is more than one drink, so free will can exist in a universe of predetermination. And because nobody is behind you forcing you to choose or making you choose and there is no compulsion, there's nothing compelling you to choose other than your ability to exercise your agency to make a choice. Your decision is made by you and you alone even though it was predetermined by God.

[Type here]

But the question of predetermination came from man-made philosophical thinking, so it is bound to be flawed. It's a kind of circular logic that progresses in a spiral that appears to give a sense of progression from the answers but the more the logic is followed the further down the spiral you travel, never really getting anyway but you think that you do because the spiral is stretched over time through the process of thought and reasoning.

In regards to the predetermined outcome some people there was never a choice because God already planned for you to make that choice, this concept but no the choice or *how you arrived at it.* This might take a while to sink in and because we have been so conditioned and manipulated to only think that there can be only one way to understand something but that is another deception. And ultimately we know that we live in a Free will universe and we know that Free Will has existed since the angels

The Angels had free will because if they didn't have free will Lucifer would not have been able to rebel with a third of

[Type here]

heaven against God. So whether a person can accept an all powerful being as God who predetermined everything and still having free will real comes down to one thing. Do you accept the bible as the final authority and truth of being?

You might ask yourself if God knows everything that's going to happen why did he allow all of this to happen? Jeremiah 29:11 :For I know the plans I have for you' declares the Lord, 'plans to prosper you and not to harm you, plans to give you hope and a future."

I challenge you to rethink your perspective and to acknowledge that if God *is* all powerful then *all of this is not allowed to happen it is happening because he wants it to happen.* All of the suffering on Earth, all of the sin, all of the death, all of the *bad things are that happened are not because he allowed it but because God wanted them to happen.* And we will see shortly how we arrive at this conclusion. The idea of man not having free will is just another way to spread confusion and deception. I bring these points up just to create a mental atmosphere within you to view things from a

[Type here]

perspective which is not conformed to churchianity in an effort to see something in a different way. Most of the suffering is because of our own actions but as long as we remain willingly ignorant, we won't hold only ourselves accountable. Romans 14:12 "So then each of us will give an account of ourselves to God".

The matter of Salvation is each person's own journey, and it is by their choices which a person will be held accountable. By saying man has no free will people are avoiding the idea that individuals hold accountability for their actions. And many people go the other way and blame Lucifer for the evils of the world. But from the beginning Lucifer's nature was to deceive, that is his role and has been from the beginning. If we search for truth, we can arrive at some interesting observations about this. If we want to get down to the truth of It Free Will is in fact the reason why evil and death exist. But it is also how man can be redeemed. So, are we redeemed by obeying God or choosing to willingly serve? If we act out of obedience it certainly isn't from love and free will but more out of a need

[Type here]

to do as we are told. If we choose to serve and believe out of love and a desire to do something because it is in the sacrifice we take joy, then we can truly be called brothers and sisters and members of the body of Christ because it is the soul of sacrifice that has taken root in us and bloomed to a point where it can bear fruit in the manifestations of "good works" in the material realm. And we can never have this seed planted unless we have accepted Jesus as Our Lord. Not only in word but in the very being of our nature down into the DNA of our being. But it is a gift ultimately a gift of God to see if we are truly worthy to receive his kingdom. If we are formed in his image and we are told to try the spirits to see if they are of God 1John4:1-5 In regard to false prophets John says "Beloved believe not every spirit but try the spirits whether they are of God". If we are told to try the spirits to see if they are of God, then God will try us to see if we are of him. In verse to John continues "hereby know ye the Spirit of God; every spirit that confesseth that Jesus is Christ come in the flesh is of God". If you have read the book this far you already know I choose to replace the word spirit with soul, because

[Type here]

God is a spirit as we have already established in scripture than it is not spirits that should be tried but the souls. 1 Peter 2:11-12 "Beloved I urge you as aliens and strangers to abstain from fleshly lusts, which wage war *against the soul*". It is not a part of the spirit that we are made a member of but his soul through the grace of God and acceptance of that grace through faith.

Ephesians 2: 8 "For by grace are ye saved through faith; and that not of yourselves: it is the gift of God: Not of works, lest any man should boast. For we are his workmanship, created in Christ Jesus unto good works, which God hath before ordained that we should walk in them."

So, does that mean we can run around and do as we please in total oblivion to how it affects others after we are joined to his soul? Obviously not. And why would you want to? Anyone who still feels the need to do what they want clearly is not a member of Christ's body.

[Type here]

The only thing we need to do is accept it. And this is not actually doing anything, it's just accepting. And to truly receive it means not being arrogant or prideful. In fact it should be humbling. Would you boast about accepting money or a gift? No, you would be prideful and boast about *having that item or possessing it.* If you have ever been given something nice, there is a feeling of embarrassment if it is noticed by someone, and they ask you where you got it. Because when you say my "mom" or "girlfriend" or someone in general gave it you it takes away from the appearance of your self-sufficiency. Being given something actually makes people have more humility but it is in their possession of it after a time that pride manifests itself.

All of these questions can really scramble the brain. Because from before the beginning we were set apart from the world. And we can't take any credit for having the desire to follow because we do it out of love and appreciation and willingness to be fulfilled by giving as our Lord Jesus joyously gave his life for us. And Jesus only did what he saw his father do. John 5;17

[Type here]

"The Son can do nothing of himself, but what he seeth the Father do: for what things soever he doeth, these also the Son do likewise". His father joyfully gave him to the world. We recognize it is a cycle of fulfillment through giving not out of some fearful dictate to obey, in fact it's the opposite. We take pleasure in serving and giving because it has been in our DNA since the beginning. Personal revelation is given to believers because it truly is not of any work or choice but from a predisposition to humble the ego and ask.

 Essentially, accepting the gift of Salvation is like winning the lottery, there is nothing you need to do to win other than just try. And the odds of winning this lottery are much greater and the payout is infinitely greater.

 I leave you with a final thought, there is a big difference between asking "Do I have to follow" and saying "please, may I follow". In these two phrasings are revealed the entirety of difference between being called and being chosen. One viewpoint only sees obeying while the other sees free will.

[Type here]

Now more than ever in the history of our World it is time to acknowledge your divine nature and be a part of the war. It is your choice and there are only two sides.

As Thomas Paine wrote "These are the times that try men's *souls*

[Type here]

www.ingramcontent.com/pod-product-compliance
Lightning Source LLC
Chambersburg PA
CBHW051824090426
42736CB00011B/1641